FAR OUTSIDE *the* ORDINARY

A MEMOIR

Prissy Elrod

Published by Leather Leaf Publishing

ISBN 978-0-9912420-0-9 (hc.)
ISBN 978-0-9912420-1-6 (pbk.)
ISBN 978-0-9912420-2-3 (ebk.)
ISBN 978-0-9912420-3-0 (aud.)

Cover design by Katie Campbell
Interior design by Jennifer Zaczek

The author has changed some names and personal details to protect the privacy of those mentioned in the book.

For Dale, who inspires me every day

~

for Garrett and Sara Britton,
my beautiful daughters and greatest accomplishment

~

for Britton, Kenley, Raynes, Allie Boone, and Whit,
who light up my life

~

for Sylvia LeBlanc Landrum, my mother,
and Mazelle Patterson, who raised me

~

and for
Jonathan Daniel Boone Kuersteiner,
whose memory lives on in the lines of this memoir

The caterpillar dies so the butterfly could be born. And, yet, the caterpillar lives in the butterfly and they are but one.
—*Unknown*

CONTENTS

Literary Disclaimer

Everyone has their own perspective, and what you read in this book is told from mine and may differ from another. I kept a personal journal during all of these events and returned to those pages when writing this memoir. I have changed some of the names but not all of them. Also, I have attempted to preserve anonymity by altering some identifying details in certain cases.

Prologue

THE DISTINGUISHED MAN OF color standing on my front porch was a sight to behold. Debonair and slim, he was a conspicuous presence. He wore a fitted silk suit. A point of pink handkerchief peaked from his jacket pocket, matching the bright pink socks that crested above his black, pointed shoes. This gentleman was the very model of cultivated elegance and charm, looking as if he had been created in Hollywood.

Somehow my tragicomedy of a story had drifted from my little panhandle town in Florida all the way west to the coast of California, where he lived. Mary Barley, my friend and personal trainer, told a friend, and that friend told *this* man, who now wanted to meet me. He wanted to hear the firsthand version directly from me.

Mary came along with him, and after formal introductions, we all sat on my pink chintz couches. I was distracted by his socks, which matched the color of my couches perfectly.

"I write for a television series called *Dawson's Creek*," he told me. "Perhaps you've seen it."

I hadn't and told him. Television hadn't been on my radar for some time.

He continued. "My position, as one of their creative writers, is to create stories and story lines. Your story intrigued me. I'd sure like to hear more about it."

It was difficult to summarize the dramatic, unimaginable, and often unbelievable events that swirled around my attempt to save my dying husband after I moved two colorful, compassionate, black caregivers into my home. There had been a constant competition between tragedy and comedy, but I found myself relaxing as I spoke to this writer. It felt good, and I was astonished to discover I could tell someone—a stranger, no less—about those dark days.

As I began to wind down my narrative, I could sense what was coming next.

"Would you consider selling your story? I think it needs to be told," Mr. Dawson's Creek said. "You tell it, we'll write it, you get paid."

Before he even asked, I knew my answer would be no. What I said, however, was, "Thank you so much for the offer. I'll get back to you."

Of course, I never did get back to him. I was afraid those I cared about might be exploited in some way. I would have no control over their reputations. Even as a bruised magnolia from the South, I cared deeply for those who cared for me.

And so, I chose to tell my own story in my own way, thirteen years after the gentleman with the wonderful pink socks came to town. The *why* was so simple. In the words of Carl Hiaasen, one of my favorite Florida authors, "You just can't make this stuff up." Mr. Dawson's Creek was right. My story really did need to be told.

PART ONE

There is nothing in a caterpillar that tells
you it's going to be a butterfly.
—*R. Buckminster Fuller*

CHAPTER ONE

Angel of Death

IT WAS SOME TIME after November 8 but before Thanksgiving. I know this because November 8 was Boone's fifty-first birthday, and I was still trying to save him. By Thanksgiving, I knew I couldn't.

The references listed for the man who was to meet me were outstanding, including names I recognized: most impressive, the late governor of Florida, LeRoy Collins, whom he'd cared for. This man had been described personally by the late governor's daughter, Mary Call, as one of twenty-eight brothers and sisters. He was said to be a gentle, kind, nurturing being.

He had schooled himself in the counsel of pain and suffering and the process of grief and bereavement. I would say he had a master's, if not his PhD, in the field of comforting and caring for others.

Wearing nicely pressed navy dress pants, shiny black shoes, and a starched white shirt, he looked as though he was interviewing for an office job rather than savior to a lost soul who was caregiver to a losing soul. His skin was marked with scars and the color of black tar. I studied his eyes, oval in shape, large and chocolate brown, the whites blemished with small red capillaries, glistening as though moisture was being blinked away. *Are they tears?* I wondered.

"My name's Cornelius, Cornelius Duhart. You can call me Du. I can help if you let me."

He knew why he was summoned and waited with quiet patience for me to speak. I remained silent. We watched each other across the room, my Southern manners absent.

Tears streamed down my face, and I began to cry. He rose from his chair and walked over and sat close. His large black arms reached out and wrapped around me. Though we were strangers, this black man held and rocked me, a fragile, scared, once fearless white woman, going through an experience so few would, or could, understand. I had yet to speak a single word.

So it went the day we met. He became known to my daughters and me as Duhart, later just Du. I was Christy, though he knew my real name was Prissy. From that day on, I saw the world differently. Sometimes seemingly unanswered prayers are answered, only in an unexpected way. The Angel of Death took residence in our home.

CHAPTER TWO

I Don't Recall

IF YOU WANT SOMETHING bad enough, there is always a way to get it. At least that was what I always thought, until that something became unattainable.

The day everything started, I was enjoying the smell of pot roast drifting downstairs from the kitchen to the room where I worked. Tired of the same old thing, I had tried a new recipe I found in *Southern Living* the day before.

I was finishing up the laundry, stacking the folded blue towels inside the empty basket. I had flunked Folding 101 but had repeated the course and become an honor's graduate: match each corner exactly, fold lengthwise in thirds, fold top to bottom once again, then stack with folded side out. Okay, I got it.

Stack. Stack. Stack.

Align said stacked towels inside the basket.

It wouldn't matter, though. I knew my husband would straighten them once I parked them in the linen closet; his eye was keener than mine.

In the background on television, Oprah was laughing with her featured guest when Boone walked in our side entrance door and startled me.

I glanced at the clock sitting on the mantel below the heirloom Daniel Boone rifle. It was only 4:15 p.m.

On any given day, Boone seldom arrived home before 11:00 p.m., and usually much later. His perfect business hours as an environmental attorney were fifteen-hour days, starting late and ending late, Monday through Friday. His guiding principle: absolutely no business on weekends, making his weekdays long, grueling, and exhausting.

I knew something was wrong when I looked up. His color was strange and ashen, his eyes large and dilated.

"What are you doing home?" I asked.

He looked confused, standing still, fixated, and staring through me. Pausing midway in folding another towel, I asked again. He still didn't answer, just stood staring.

"Why won't you answer me?"

"I don't recall."

"You don't recall what?"

"I don't recall how I got here. I couldn't find my way. There was a tall building."

"What are you talking about? Where's your car?"

"I don't recall."

I swept past him through the side door and saw his black Suburban sitting in our driveway, parked at an angle, the front fender lurching over the manicured boxwoods. The driver's door was open; the engine was still running.

Stunned, I turned off the ignition and left the car parked crooked. Too worried to care, I ran back inside. Boone was still standing, but now swaying. He didn't drink, so I knew he wasn't drunk.

I eased him down on our worn, slipcovered sofa. I'd dressed that sofa in so many different covers it could have been my Barbie doll. Today it was wearing red and white ticking, the contrast making Boone look whiter than a ghost.

I left him sitting and sprinted upstairs to the kitchen—thinking, *hypoglycemia.*

As a physician's daughter, I'd spent years preaching my opinions to others, whether they were interested or not, endorsing homeopathic treatments and alternative medicine. It was as though I had actual training and confirmed knowledge in every field of medicine. Most times, I even believed myself. "Those Landrum girls are the last living authority on everything they know nothing about," my brother-in-law regularly gibed, referring to my mother, my sisters, and me as well.

I grabbed a Coke and some crackers and hurried back to Boone. I handed him the crackers, urging him to eat. In between his nibbles and sips I questioned him.

"What's my name?" I asked.

"I'm not sure."

I swallowed. It felt as though something was stuck in my throat. "How many children do we have?"

He guessed wrong. My heart was barely a beat from tachycardia when I began considering my own diagnosis for him: embolism or stroke.

"I'm calling an ambulance."

"*No* ambulance. Just give me a minute."

At least he knows what an ambulance is, I thought. His color seemed to be returning, maybe because he'd ingested some calories.

"You must be dehydrated. Have you eaten anything today?" I began dialing Alex, Boone's best friend. Alex was an obstetrician, but I still thought he'd know what to do.

"Hang up the phone. Don't call anyone," Boone yelled from the sofa.

When Alex answered, I whispered into the receiver. "Something's wrong with Boone," I said. "Something weird, a stroke maybe."

"What? Call an ambulance, Prissy. I'm on my way." He hung up before I could say another word. I tried dialing 911.

Boone watched, stumbled over, grabbed the receiver, then tossed it to the floor. "No ambulance," he said.

Alex arrived within fifteen minutes, but the ambulance never did. No coercion from either one of us could persuade Boone to let us call for one.

Alex checked him over, and Boone seemed better. Still, Alex called and talked to the neurologist on call at the hospital. The neurologist suggested we transport Boone to the ER right away. Boone argued, adamantly refused, and finally we gave up.

Boone was like that. When he dug his heels in, there was no changing his mind. Thirty minutes later he seemed normal, or himself, I should say. The three of us sat around eating boiled peanuts as though nothing had happened.

In retrospect, everything that happened that day was so uncharacteristic of Boone, but I was blind to the red flags.

He was a man who worried about everything, even a benign mole. Our children's delicate skin was scarred from the needless removal of suspicious moles spotted by Boone's watchful eyes. He wanted them safe. "No moles on my children," he told the plastic surgeon.

It was October. The first crisp air of fall had stretched its toes down from Canada to Florida, brushing the leaves, their color transformed from a kaleidoscope of summer greens to a fall palette of persimmon, ochre, and sienna. It was my favorite season, and I was a Pollyanna by nature. Maybe that was why I convinced myself this incident was a one-time thing. *He should avoid skipping meals and chewing his nasty tobacco*, I thought. A vice inherited along with his love of hunting, the connection unexplainable but regularly accepted in the South.

The holidays of November and December came and went. I gave little thought to that autumn day when my husband, after twenty-four years of marriage, didn't even recall my name.

CHAPTER THREE

A Wing of Protection

I PUT THE INCIDENT behind me and became preoccupied as we moved through the holidays. We were a few days into January, and our nineteen-year-old daughter, Garrett, was still home for Christmas break from the University of Alabama. She planned to head back the next day for the second semester. Her car was already packed full to the brim.

She and I spent most of the afternoon dismantling the Christmas tree. We wrapped, boxed, and stored all the cherished ornaments we'd collected over the years. Both of us exhausted, we lounged on the couch watching television, her head resting on my lap, our poodles nestled on each side of her. Boone and our sixteen-year-old daughter, Sara Britton, had gone to a horse show in Gainesville, a nearby city.

"Mom, I don't want to go back," she whispered, barely audible.

"Back where?" I asked, engrossed in *Law and Order*.

"Alabama. I think I'm going to stay here, go to FSU."

"What?" I lifted her head off my lap and punched off the remote. "What's going on?"

"I don't know. I really don't. I just want to stay here and go to FSU. I can't explain why. I don't even know why. I just do. It feels right."

"Then okay. That's what you should do."

I had been urging her to transfer for the last seven months. I had wanted her to enroll at Florida State University in our hometown ever since the end of her freshman year at Alabama, a day that had etched a memory in my brain I would never forget.

On a day beautiful day in May, just before the start of summer, I called Garrett. Her last exam was over, the sorority house closed, and most of her friends had gone home. She was more than ready to vacate Tuscaloosa, having spent half of her first year there homesick. She planned to empty her dorm room, load everything into her Jeep, and drive home the next day. I always worried about her driving alone on the lone country roads between the two cities of Tuscaloosa and Tallahassee.

"You think everything will fit in your car?" I asked.

"I'm not sure. Probably—I think so. It'll be packed pretty tight, though."

"Maybe I should come up and help you empty the room. We could load some of it in my Jeep. I could follow you home."

"That's a great idea. Would you want to do that?" She sounded happy and offered to make dinner reservations for our night in Tuscaloosa.

And so it was planned. I took my sister Deborah with me the next day, and we drove to Alabama. As soon as we arrived, we emptied what was left inside Garrett's dorm room and packed both cars. Later, we shared a meal at a local restaurant and piled together in one room at the local motel, all of us exhausted, for a good night's sleep.

Early the next day, the weather perfect, we began our caravan toward Tallahassee. Garrett took the lead, and we followed close behind: two Jeep Cherokees, a two-lane highway, little traffic, and very few houses spotting the landscape.

It happened in an instant, only two hours into the trip.

I watched a Jeep run off the road, swerve back, and go airborne. There was one summersault, and another summersault. The contrast—a black object spinning, centered in blue sky—momentarily confused me.

"Look, Deborah. That car is flipping," I said, not comprehending it was my own daughter in the air as I drove fifty-five miles per hour, stupefied.

"Oh my God, it's Garrett!" she screamed.

I watched the car land upside down on the other side of the road, across from the oncoming traffic. As my brain registered the horror, I tried to get out of my seat belt and open the door even though my Jeep was still traveling forty to fifty miles per hour.

Deborah screamed again. "Stop the car! Stop the car!" She grabbed the steering wheel and helped me pull off the road.

I bolted from the car and ran toward the Jeep, screaming, "Garrett, please God. Where are you, Garrett?"

I was praying for mercy as I looked at the crumbled wreckage. The car didn't even look familiar—upside down, the four wheels still spinning in the air. Where was the driver's side? I couldn't find it.

I was crawling on my hands and knees, disoriented. The sandspurs pierced my bare knees as the overgrown weeds slapped my face, wet from snot and tears. I was crawling in circles, trying to find my child, screaming her name. In the background, I heard sirens.

I thought I heard a whisper, a faint voice. I listened again, holding my breath.

"Mom, help me."

I crawled toward the sound and found her dangling upside down in her seat belt, hanging from her seat. I climbed into the crushed steel and through the broken window, moved toward her and unclasped the seat belt, then pulled her out through the absent window. I was sobbing, clinging, and still praying out loud.

"I'm okay, Momma. I'm okay." She was talking. She was moving. She was alive. She cried as I held her. She hadn't called me "Momma" in years.

The first responders and "Jaws of Life" arrived, along with three fire trucks and an ambulance. A firefighters' cookout was in progress down the road, so they were all there in minutes. The sheriff's deputies arrived soon afterward.

"Holy crap, where's the victim?" I heard a deputy ask one of the first responders, who pointed to Garrett still wrapped in my arms.

"No damn way. I can't believe that, man."

It was unfathomable to everyone staring at the black pile, its top crushed into the front leather seats. By then, reality had sunk in for me. I was put into the ambulance while the officials tried to piece together what happened. I heard someone mention a house up the road.

"Let me see if anyone saw what happened," one of the deputies said over his shoulder as he walked away.

Garrett explained her recollection to the other deputy as he scribbled on a pad. I listened, still mute in the ambulance with a blood pressure cuff around my arm.

"I was changing my CD and looked down, but just for a second," Garrett explained. "I ran off the road then tried to get back on, but I turned the wheel too hard, maybe because it scared me. Anyway, then it started to flip. I dropped my head and shut my eyes and let go of the wheel, I think. My head was down, but I saw blue sky, so I must have opened my eyes."

"You overcompensated," I heard him say.

Twenty minutes later the other deputy came back from his visit to the house where he'd gone looking for a witness. He found one—an old black man sitting on his front porch. He'd told the sheriff he sat there all day, almost every day. He liked to watch the cars go by. He saw the whole thing, just how it happened.

"I see that car yonder." He pointed toward the pile of crushed metal. "It coming down the road. I seen this white thing, look to me like a wing, hanged out the other side. I believe I seen an angel wing. Sho do. It sho was."

"Did you ask where he kept his moonshine?" I heard one of the first responders say, laughing.

But I believed him, I did. How else could one explain her survival without even a scratch? It was a miracle.

The firemen transferred all the stuff from Garrett's Jeep to mine. Garrett climbed in the passenger seat, and Deborah volunteered to drive. We left the scene three hours after impact. Inside Garrett's Vera Bradley duffel bag on the backseat floor, I found a bottle of unopened bourbon. I drank it straight from the bottle the minute we were out of the deputies' sight.

The insurance company considered the car destroyed and issued a check for the current value. When we received the check the next week, we bought her the same exact car. If it wasn't an angel that saved her, I believed her model had to be the safest car on the planet.

I changed after that day. My faith, already strong, was more profound. I had a gratifying belief in the impossible. It wasn't really a spiritual awakening but more a blind trust in miracles.

So, no matter her reasons, when Garrett said she didn't want to go back to Alabama, I was ecstatic. I just needed to figure out how to tell her dad, especially since he had already paid the nonrefundable tuition.

I never told Garrett there was a moment in time only a few weeks earlier when her father didn't even remember he had a daughter, much less one who attended the University of Alabama and wanted to transfer home for reasons unknown to even her.

CHAPTER FOUR

Dr. Doom

On a cold February day nine months after Garrett's automobile accident, the temperature had dropped into the single digits, uncommon for the panhandle of Florida. A curtain of threatening clouds lingered over the steel-gray sky.

Boone and I were in Jacksonville, returning to the Mayo Clinic for a consultation and final summary of his test results after his routine physical the day before. It was his annual visit, always done in February. I liked going along to shop and joined him for the overnight trip.

The discharging physician was reviewing the summary of tests. I sat quietly in the spare chair listening. Everything was normal, a few findings better than normal. He dutifully suggested Boone keep up the good work, confirming he would see him the following year.

Performing the customary handshake with cordial pleasantries—a smile, a thank-you, and a goodbye—we turned to leave. Boone's hand was brushing the small of my back, escorting me closer to the door.

I turned around. "Did he mention the day he forgot who I was?"

The doctor's smile faded.

Boone had specifically asked me not to mention what happened that day in October, only four months earlier. Good lawyers are great arguers, so his reasons made perfect sense to me. He was working on a big case: ValuJet Flight 592, which, less than a year ago, on May 11, 1996, had crashed into the Everglades, killing all 110 people aboard. In the eyes of a perfectionist like Boone, any memory difficulty was imperfection and not acceptable. He didn't want negative exposure impacting legal participation on any of his cases, particularly this one.

The doctor was not as complacent. He ordered multiple tests, assuring us both that it was a routine precaution.

Five hours later, we found ourselves waiting outside radiology, where a three-hour memory test and a two-hour MRI had been performed.

Boone had recently been having headaches, which was unusual for him. As we continued to wait in the uncomfortable chairs outside the diagnostic room, I recalled a conversation between us a few weeks earlier.

"Do you think I could have a brain tumor?" he asked me out of the blue.

I was getting ready to meet some girlfriends for dinner. "You're so dramatic," I said. "Everyone has headaches." I rolled my eyes and finished applying my bronze lipstick.

I heard the radiologist talking on the phone through the thin wall. "I can't let him leave here and just drive off," he was telling someone. "He shouldn't be behind the wheel of a car."

"Who are they talking about?" Boone asked me, looking panicked.

My mind began formulating an answer. "I heard the man's name, Jack somebody," I told him. "It wasn't you."

I couldn't breathe. Why had I not been more aware? In that moment I began feeling a wave of smothering guilt and negligence, as though I were responsible. *What if it really* was *something?* My heart was beating so loud Boone had to hear it.

I slid my sweaty palms under my buttocks and sat on them, waiting for the door to open. A stranger wearing a starched white lab coat, his unfamiliar name embroidered above the pocket, walked in. I noticed he wasn't looking at us but down, toward the floor. I knew before he even looked up that his words would change our world forever.

The radiologist, "Dr. Doom," I called him, had found a large shadowing in the center core of Boone's brain. Suspecting a tumor, he suggested we meet with neurosurgeons the following day to better understand the ramifications. Dr. Doom could not tell us if it was operable and certainly wished he had better news.

The room spun. It seemed as though the temperature changed in an instant, first freezing cold, then hot, then freezing cold again. My heart somersaulted with my stomach; my eyes lost focus; my hearing seized; my throat constricted. We were immersed in the unknown, a purgatory. I began to shake as though I were sitting in a tub of ice, my teeth chattering. I heard this stranger talking but was no longer listening to anything he said.

Our fingers laced together tightly as we silently walked through the quiet corridor. I observed the unscathed people collecting their things, talking and smiling, some laughing, their shifts over.

It is an oddity many traumatized victims realize during a crisis. Life changes only for the wounded, those directly hit. There was a line between us now. They were normal; we weren't.

We stepped out the door into the cold February night. Sunlight had long ago faded. There was no cow jumping over the moon. There were only two or three cars left in the dark parking lot. The clinic had been closed for over an hour. We were the last patients.

We sat in our car shell-shocked, surrounded by the frivolous magazines I had so casually enjoyed only hours before. We were three hours away from family, friends, or any zone of comfort we knew.

"I need you to do something for me," Boone said, looking forward into the night.

"What?" I was swallowing a cry, on the verge of a sob.

"When we get home, I want you to get all the guns out of the house."

"My God . . . why would you even say something like that?" I started to cry.

"Just do it, please. I don't want to do something stupid."

I realized his sense of hopelessness had already seeded. I knew our roles had reversed in the blink of an eye. I'd been given the unwanted, unsolicited title of CCC: CEO, CFO, and Caregiver of our once ideal and now shattered life. My most important role as a human being was about to be tested with no way to study or prepare.

That very night, I began the arduous search for the end of the rainbow, praying it would be filled with hope rather than the fabled pot of gold.

CHAPTER FIVE

Dog With a Bone

I NEVER WAS ONE to take no for an answer, not when there was a chance for yes. I always believed that with careful thought, planning, and action, just about anything could be created, improved, or solved. In other words, when my mind was made up about something, I was like a dog with a bone. I'd sniff an idea, paw it, circle it, and bury it. Later, I'd dig it up, taste it, and maybe bury it again. Finally, I'd dig that bone up and chew and chew, sometimes for a very long time.

I began gnawing on my first bone in my twenties. I wanted to wear designer clothes but had no money or means to buy them. But I wanted them so badly I had to find a way.

I researched, found, interviewed, and decided to work for Doncaster, a unique designer clothing company in North Carolina, which based all of their sales and marketing in non-storefront settings—the homes of housewives.

It was perfect, just what I was looking for, since I had a newborn at the time. It was strictly commission; the more I sold, the more I earned. My friend Inez was already employed by the company. I called her and asked to partner with her.

We would unpack the massive trunks, display the clothes—hanging them from windows and doors all over my house—and then call and invite friends to come over at an appointed time between 9:00 a.m. and 9:00 p.m.

In between feeding my baby and changing her diapers, I sold the clothes, arranged alterations, personally delivered and invoiced orders, and then collected the money. I'd repack the clothes into the same multiple trunks, load them into the car, and drive to the next waiting housewife—sometimes in another state—in my oversized Oldsmobile station wagon. I chewed on that bone for twenty-five years. I even had a calling card with a title engraved on it: Fashion Consultant.

The second bone I stumbled across in my thirties. I had two young daughters by then and was still chewing the first bone. But I craved a new flavor: this time, oil-painted portraits.

When I was a young child, my mother commissioned a portrait artist to paint old-world-style paintings of my sisters and me; they still hung in my mother's house. Wanting the same for both my daughters, I located the same artist who'd painted my sisters and me. He lived in Birmingham. I urged him to come to Tallahassee and paint my daughter Garrett's portrait.

I had no money for such an extravagant purchase, so I bartered. In exchange for his travel, I agreed to contract four of my friends to have their children's portraits painted as well. He agreed and offered to pay a commission for my efforts. It was the beginning of our fifteen-year business. I made enough commission to pay for much more than portraits. I was chewing two bones at the same time, with two different flavors. I liked it. I had another calling card printed and a new title embossed: Portrait Consultant.

A decade passed. I was turning forty and had another craving. I didn't really want to bury my old bones, but my palette had a hankering for something different—an appetite for travel. I didn't really care where I went. After all, I was a dog with a bone. Just put me in the backseat and roll down the windows. I was happy to go anywhere.

As usual, we were back to the same old song, just different lyrics: not enough money. No worry, I would turn it into a job, then it couldn't be labeled pleasure. I would be "working," not just traveling. Boone would have no trouble with my absence from household responsibilities if I were working.

I withheld my newest harebrained scheme from Boone until I had the deal sealed. I circled, scratched, and pawed until I found the perfect travel agent to share my new bone: "Girls' Getaway to New York City" for shopping, theater, and Christmas festivities. I would plan it for the weekend after Thanksgiving. My idea sounded appetizing to the agent, and he wanted a taste. Also, I wouldn't be working inside his office with my minimal computer experience but outside as a commissioned sales representative. What could he lose, right?

"Prissy, I swear, you could sell fleas to a dog," my friend Gayle said when I told her my news.

"Don't you get it? I am the dog."

I capped my quota at twenty-five clients per trip. Turned out, I was hugely successful at planning, organizing, booking, directing, and escorting. The trips sold out three or four days after my flyers circulated.

After several years and many Radio City Music Hall follies, I was feeling my confidence and broadened my scope to Europe and Asia, escorting my flock like a sheep with her lambs. My clients became my friends; my friends became my clients. It looked like I had another delicious bone to chew—free travel. It meant another calling card to print: Travel Consultant.

I thought myself so clever, ingenious, creative, stubborn, and worldly that I could solve anything. I had yet to learn my superficial desires were incidental. The real and most important longings were beyond my reach, or anyone else's.

CHAPTER SIX

Dr. Mean

I WASTED NO TIME locating him in *U.S. News and World Report*'s *Best Hospitals* rankings magazine, which had been released a few months earlier. I thought any medical center making the cut must have great surgeons. One doctor was at the top of the list and only two hours away. We anxiously awaited the scheduled appointment and finally the day came for our trip to Gainesville, though our insurance provider had yet to approve our request for a second opinion.

In fact, an hour before Boone was rolled into the operating room, he still had not been approved by our health care provider. It was only after one of Boone's law partners, Ron, made a personal call to the insurance company's CEO on Boone's behalf that the paperwork—still pending—finally went through. We were fortunate that Ron happened to legally represent our particular insurance company. Maybe, just maybe, good luck was on our side. I hoped.

I was visibly shaken and drained from the recent days' events, and Boone was completely silent. As we cowered together in the cold, sterile room, we listened. The neurosurgeon, a.k.a. Dr. Mean, was brutally frank from the moment he met us: curt, swift, and aloof. His bedside manner was scathing as he flexed his medical muscles, scanning the films I handed over to him copied from the Mayo Clinic.

He called it a glioblastoma multiforme, stage IV. It had the nickname "glio," which sounded less threatening than the real name. It was one of the most fatal forms of brain tumors, targeting mostly men usually between the ages of fifty and sixty-four. Boone had turned fifty only three months before.

The doctor thought he could remove most of the tumor, though the procedure was life threatening. He couldn't promise survival from the surgery, based on the location of the tumor. He couldn't guarantee what residual effects might occur from the complicated surgery. What he could guarantee: it was fast growing, deadly, and terminal. Bang. Just like that.

I made excuses for such an unsympathetic and blunt dialogue. *He is gifted, highly regarded, and sought after, affording him this abrupt and unfriendly demeanor*, I thought. Later, I would decide he was just plain old rude and arrogant.

As Boone fought for his life during the seven hours of surgery, I was remembering a time nine years earlier, when another man I loved battled brain cancer—my beloved father. I wondered how two men in my life could succumb to the same disease. What were the odds?

My daughters and I waited, surrounded by a village of family and friends filling most of the chairs in the large surgical waiting room. When Dr. Mean finally appeared, there was a quiet hush among everyone as he walked toward us. I held my daughters' hands; we waited for his words. His eyebrows glistened with sweat, his blue scrubs a shade darker from perspiration, the smears of dried blood blotched over blue: Boone's blood. His manner was beyond solemn.

"He survived. Removed 99 percent of the tumor," he said.

My heart leapt, all three of us crying openly. I was about to thank him, but before I could, Dr. Mean continued. "If you do nothing, he won't live more than three months, I'm afraid. But, if we radiate, he could live a year. That's the best you can hope for. I'm really sorry. I really am."

He patted my arm and asked if I had any questions but wasn't really waiting to listen. I was too dazed to ask anything.

He turned around and walked away, on to his next hopeless case, I suspected.

I gazed with panicked shock at family and friends occupying all the waiting room chairs and looked for Mazelle, the only one who might be able to comfort me. I made my way over to her, and she pulled me into her familiar black arms. I crawled into her lap, cradled my face into her neck, and wept.

I listened as she whispered, "Hush, baby girl, it gone be all right." I was forty-six years old, and I believed her.

Mazelle had rocked me as a baby and embraced and nurtured me as a child. When I was a teenager, she scolded, punished, and supported me. Even though I was now an adult, she continued to mentor me. She taught my sisters and me right from wrong, empathy, sympathy, consideration, and all the characteristics I believe make a person likable, respectable, and successful.

With only an eighth-grade education, Mazelle could tell you anything you wanted to know about the Bible. She taught herself how to upholster furniture and create magnificent wedding cakes, and she could cook her way around any master chef.

She had been a kindred soul through my happiest and darkest hours. When I brought my babies home from the hospital, she was waiting for me, having driven the hundred-mile distance from her home to mine. She stayed those first scary days and nights, showing me the ways to touch and love my newborn. Those were my happiest hours. I felt privileged to have been part of her life for all of my life.

Woven into our family like an heirloom quilt, in another time, Mazelle Patterson would have been called domestic help. She was part of our family before I was born, awaiting me—a five-pound nothing—to arrive home from the hospital. Seventy-five years old, she had driven herself the sixty miles to the hospital and waited, along with everyone else, during Boone's surgery. Though I'm sure my weight grew heavy, I continued to sit in her lap as she quietly held me and listened to me crying.

Boone's attitude following his surgery was remarkable. When he awoke the next day, he was so happy just to be alive. He never believed he would survive, or if he did, feared he would be left in a vegetative state.

By his second day in recovery, Boone had learned everyone's name who walked through the door: nurses to housekeeping, lab technicians to respiratory therapists, neurosurgeons to oncologists. He wanted to know all about them. And not just them, but their entire family and life history. He offered our beach house to the sweet lady emptying the trash.

"Take your whole family to our house; there's plenty of room. Invite them all," he offered while I sat mute. At least fifteen different people in the course of a week had been invited to take their vacation at our beach house.

"We don't mind, right, Prissy? They can bring whoever they want," he kept saying over and over to anyone and everyone.

I kept nodding my head up and down. "Yes, of course. You are welcome to come," I replied.

Following his discharge from the hospital, we stayed in Gainesville awaiting his follow-up visit scheduled for three days later. Boone was jogging around the University of Florida campus one week after his craniotomy, a stitched and jagged eight-inch battle wound clearly visible on his shaved head. Yet, he was still happy.

Since he needed to heal before starting his radiation treatments, we soon traveled back to Tallahassee for his recuperation. He was still euphoric, hopeful, and chatty. I knew he was never one to just sit, read, and relax. It wasn't in his DNA. He needed a project. Even more, I needed him to have a project.

My good friend Lucki dropped in to visit the afternoon we arrived home from Gainesville. We had been neighbors for almost two decades; her daughters had helped raise my own two daughters, constantly babysitting for me. Lucki and I had a very special bond for two reasons: First, she was a hoot, more fun than just about anyone I knew. Second, and now even more important, her husband also had had a brain tumor. George battled his war and lost as Boone and I watched from the sidelines. Lucki knew what we were going through and what lay ahead. We had lived directly across the street from each other for seventeen years. Neither one of us could believe that George and Boone, both young men, in their fifties, had been diagnosed with brain tumors on a street with only nine houses. The statistical odds seemed staggering to us, as well as to everyone who knew us.

Lucki had suggested Boone organize our daughters' collections of childhood treasures—my treasures, really. I had saved every scrap of artwork, love note, report card, class picture, ribbon, trophy, certificate of honor, and everything in between since the day each was born. They were sixteen and twenty years old at the time. Boone started his newfound project the very next day.

In a week's time, he had five huge bins complete, not just for the girls, but for us as well. Our names were scribbled on the plastic lids in indelible ink: Boone, Prissy, Garrett, and Sara Britton. The fifth bin said "Family" and held pictures from vacations, Christmases, Easters, parties, birthdays, and more, all in chronological order. It was simply incredible but not surprising to me. He not only was a perfectionist but also had an obsessive-compulsive personality disorder. No one could know what that really means unless they have lived with someone who really is.

CHAPTER SEVEN

Boone

MORE OFTEN THAN NOT, opposites attract, and Boone and I were complete opposites. In retrospect, I'm sure he thought he could change me, just as I thought I could change him. Both of us were disappointed to learn that rarely—well, never—does it work like that. Still, neither one of us ever gave up trying. He was the Brook Brothers' type, and I, in my heart and style, was more the Pippi Longstocking type. I would have loved nothing more than to wear some laced combat boots to the Tallahassee Junior League meeting but kept the urge to buy and wear them parked in my heart. I was the middle of three daughters and thus carried the pleasing gene. I dressed the conservative part to make Boone happy.

I have a Rule of Columns that I've used for many years with people, purchases, employment, and life. I draw a vertical line down the middle of a page. On the left side, I put good qualities, attributes, and assets. On the right side, I put bad qualities, flaws, and liabilities. If the left side exceeds the right, I might overlook a few things on the right. After all, no one is perfect.

Although Boone had many wonderful qualities that filled my rule list when we first met, as the years passed, his worst quality—his OCD—seemed to swell. He liked things done with perfection, neatly, and in order. I knew this about him before I married him. However, in my Rule of Columns, his left side far outweighed the right, which listed "perfectionist."

Boone wanted everyone and everything around him perfect. Yet he lived in an imperfect world with a bunch of imperfect people. This was always a struggle for him, me, and us.

A champion of hunting, fishing, and gardening, Boone had a great passion for digging up pottery and arrowheads on Turkey Point, a beautiful spot near the Gulf of Mexico. We had a small house on the beach in St. Teresa, close to Tallahassee. Each morning there, Boone would take his small paddleboat and spend hours searching, digging, and collecting archeological riches: arrowheads and old remnants of bowls and cups. He would bring his treasures home and triple-clean them. It was hard to bring sparkle to something hundreds of years old. Even so, Boone would try.

When you live with someone who expects perfection, life is easier if you just enlist yourself, even if as a hostile participant. It was really that simple. I never liked confrontation of any kind, so I became his apprentice in the school of perfection. It would take me years to learn all he wanted me to know. When I finally did, I realized I never wanted the degree. I knew there was no such thing as perfect.

Here is what you find when you visit the mind of an amateur perfectionist like me, after years of being Boone's apprentice.

It is eight o'clock in the morning on a typical day. I make a cup of coffee and look forward to sitting down and watching the *Today* show. I see the pillows are not fluffed or are out of order—order being three on one side of the couch and three on the other side, their colors coordinated just right. Whoops, there are white athletic socks on the floor under the coffee table. First, I arrange the pillows; if not, how can I sit and relax? I take the socks to the laundry room but find other dirty clothes not sorted. I sort. There are three piles since only yesterday, yet only two people living in our house, so I start the wash. How can only two people create three piles in one day? Simple answer—me. A bath towel, hand towel, and washcloth are only used once then washed, according to me. The same goes for clothes.

Okay, the washer is going, so I go back to the coffee, which is getting colder, but then remember I should make sure there are no other clothes in the laundry hamper that should also be washed. Back to the bedroom I go to check for them and remember I have not made the bed. I must make it. While getting the clothes to add to the washing machine, I see the water glasses next to the bed; they need to go to the kitchen. Carrying the extra laundry, along with the glasses, I march to the laundry room by way of the kitchen. Oh no, there are other dishes in the sink; they need to be loaded into the dishwasher. I will do that but after I take this laundry and put it in the already-turned-on washing machine. They are white, so they must go in with the other whites.

Back to the kitchen now, I have to load those dishes right away. Letting them sit there for another ten minutes would just annoy me, and I would not enjoy my coffee. I load.

I go back to the couch to sit down, and my coffee is ice cold. It has taken me forty-five minutes to sit and enjoy my first sip, and it is only the first hour of my day.

Herein lies the problem: this learned behavior is very difficult to unlearn. It is like someone has tarred you, and there's no dissolvent in the world to remove it.

Perfection paralyzes people, robbing them of valuable time, which to me is greater than the value of money. A person seeking perfection struggles with change. It is as much an addiction as alcohol, drugs, or sex and just as crippling as bulimia or anorexia.

You realize it is ridiculous behavior, but it compels you, nonetheless. When the demons of disarray tiptoe into my consciousness, it is as tiresome as a nagging headache. Reaching for an aspirin won't remedy it, though.

This might have been considered small stuff when I first enrolled in Boone's school of perfectionism years ago. It doesn't seem small now.

I think an overly ordered mind comes with a huge price. What a perfectionist sees is only imperfection, in every detail.

Flawless strife for perfection in a blemished world will ultimately crush your spirit. I think the circumstances were showing us that.

My poor daughters had to hear about my Rule of Columns throughout their teen years when choosing friends. Boyfriends especially got the dissection. When we finished with those boys, it narrowed the pickings for choosing prized husbands. Few good boys were left.

I had my Rules of Mention engrained in them as well; they were of merit and not debatable. Choose a man who respects his mother if you want him to respect you. Of course, anyone would know this, but I continued to preach it anyway.

Finally, last but certainly not least, there's my Rule of Three. I would preach this to single girlfriends. Give someone three dates. It's unfair to judge a person on one date, unless they are a rapist, a drunk, or a felon.

The first date is shallow and superficial. It's all about looks, clothes, and clean fingernails. Moving on, the second date is interests, passions, personality, character, and attraction. The third is the important date. This is about the person, no matter their looks, fashion, or social wealth. It is the very core of what really matters and where you determine if there is moral fiber threading through them.

You can usually tell by this point; at least I could. After the third date, it's time to reel them in or cut them loose. My Rule of Three has given blood to more than one anemic loner. It also gave me Boone.

CHAPTER EIGHT

Flicker of Luck

ONCE BOONE SURVIVED SURGERY, he needed intensive radiation, so we opted to temporarily move to an apartment near the hospital, two hours away in Gainesville. We packed our bags, hired a house-, child-, and pet-sitter, as well as a bookkeeper, and then drove off.

For six weeks, twice a day, five days a week, his brain was radiated as I sat in the waiting room watching hopeful cancer patients in their blue gowns shuffle around me, all marked with Xs—bull's-eye targets for their zaps.

From the first treatment Boone was sick. Any smells—food, fabric, or fellow—would cause him to vomit. The oncologist said Boone's nausea was worse than most other cancer patients and suggested an anti-nausea drug generally prescribed for HIV patients. I picked up the uninsured prescription and paid the $1,000. It didn't help. Of course, they wouldn't give me a refund. So, with only one pill used, I threw them away.

As Boone's weight dropped, so did mine. I wanted to eat, but any smell made it worse for him. I resolved to drink Ensure, a supplement drink. I consumed it sitting outside the door of our apartment so he couldn't smell it.

When our family came to visit, we would venture to a restaurant. I could see the anguish in Boone's eyes throughout dinner, making even that meal unpalatable for me.

During those six weeks that we lived in Gainesville as he underwent the twice-daily radiation, I wasted no time searching to find answers, researching any alternative cures, remedies, following up on leads, and calling strangers who were receiving treatments for their terminal illnesses and asking them personal questions: What are you taking, doing, eating, supplementing? Nothing was sacred to me, and nothing seemed too personal in my quest to find answers.

I decided to befriend the oncologist treating Boone, whom I named Dr. Care, and invited him and his wife out to dinner. I hoped he would see us as friends, not just another patient piled in his stack. I was surprised when he accepted.

During the dinner, Boone was crippled with exhaustion and nausea but swallowed his urge to vomit. He was silent throughout the meal. After the salad plates were cleared, I started grilling Dr. Care about his surviving patients, ones with Boone's particular disease.

I had to know what they might be doing differently, what we could do better. He divulged nothing and tried to change the subject while his wife sat silent and dumbfounded, her food uneaten. I suppose, looking back, I was shameless.

My endeavor was successful, though. The next day, Dr. Care called me. He had contacted his longest-surviving patient with a glioblastoma and asked if she might speak with me. He'd given her my phone number. I dared imagine what he told her about me. I waited for her call.

In the meantime, I researched a Chinese foot soak I'd read about. Their guarantee convinced me the herbs would travel from Boone's feet, soaked in a plastic container filled with purple slush, all the way to his brain, where the tumor would miraculously dissolve. Okay, I was skeptical. Even chemotherapy wasn't a recommended treatment because of the blood-brain barrier. But they gave a guarantee. *Would they really lie about it and offer to give the money back?*

Before ordering the magic potion, I did more research, I really did. I actually called strangers who were also dying and on the

the treatment to see if they were doing better. The names were given to me by the company, so of course they were doing better. They were probably employees sitting in a third-world country making the potion. No surprise, I was scammed.

When you feel suffocated by hopelessness, you are willing to gamble anything. Money is the least of your worries. Boone never once put his feet in my prepared tub. The vile smell that lifted from the crap filling the pan permeated our rented apartment. He vomited for two days. A few weeks later, the $900 purchase appeared on my credit card. I called to complain. The number had been disconnected, and the crooks had fled.

A week later, Dr. Care's longest-surviving patient—seven years and counting—called me. I was overjoyed. Her name was Sue. She lived only an hour away from where we stayed and offered to drive over and meet us the following day. I was making my list of questions to ask her. I slipped out later to buy her a gift of gratitude.

The next day, we drove the short distance to the Olive Garden. I was certain Sue would have the answers and be willing to share her magic formula, shining the light of life our way. We were nervous, as if we were going to meet a rock star rather than a cancer survivor.

"What do you think we should ask?" Boone wanted to know, believing she could have the equivalent of a winning lottery ticket.

I gently smoothed an unruly strand of thinning hair from his forehead, realizing the radiation had begun its transformation. "Don't worry. I know what to ask."

After the waitress seated us, I left Boone and went up front to wait for Sue, wanting to meet and greet her myself before Boone met her. I really didn't know who I was looking for, since we hadn't exchanged descriptions. I assumed she would be thin and vegan looking, probably from eating only organic foods grown on her own farm. She probably shopped at the local health food store and had bought an arsenal of lifesaving supplements. We could do that. We would do that.

I was watching out the window and noticed a cigarette flying through the air when a motorcycle scooted into a vacant parking spot. Anxiously awaiting Sue, I continued to scan outside, watching person after person exit their cars. A few minutes later, I was tapped on my shoulder.

"Are you Prissy?"

I turned around to meet Sue, but not the Sue I imagined, not a vegan Sue or a healthy-looking Sue. Standing before me was a woman nearing three hundred pounds and covered with tattoos. She had ridden her motorcycle—without a helmet—and was the one who had flicked the finished cigarette into the air.

I knew my list of questions was worthless, but after joining Boone at the table, I decided I should ask them anyway. She sat directly across from us as I pulled out my list.

"Are you taking any vitamins or supplements? What about yoga and meditation? Acupuncture? Do you have a special diet?" I asked one question after another, watching her as she shook her head left to right, a no to each of my questions. Her sympathetic eyes locked with Boone's. He said nothing as his wishful hazel eyes stared back at her.

Her small statistical survival was based on just plain old luck. I knew we were on our own before we ever ordered our food.

CHAPTER NINE

Loss of Innocence

FINALLY, RADIATION CAMP WAS over. Boone was discharged from the cancer center and instructed to return in May for another MRI. Thin, tired, and homesick, we packed our bags, along with the carload of relocation gear, and headed north then west, toward home. We missed our daughters, our families, our friends, even Puddles and Pooh, our teacup poodles.

Although the weeks had been difficult, I tried to remain positive, believing all the radiation must have eradicated any residual cancer. It was a mystery to me how any cell could survive the regimen Boone had endured. The precise aim toward a marked X had been targeted twice a day for thirty days. That was sixty times, for God's sake. Surely, every single tentacle lurking or hiding must be gone.

Three hours later, when we arrived home, we walked in the back door to find that two of our closest friends were waiting for us, along with our girls. Our friends had filled our home with bouquets of flowers: roses, snapdragons, sweet pea, and lily of the valley, their vibrant shades of pink, crimson, pure white, and pink-and-white delicately flocked together in perfect vases, adding vibrant beauty to every room. We were transfixed, lost in the intoxicating perfume, which swept away the antiseptic smell still lingering in our clothes and hair.

Our daughters had vacuumed away all dust particles and shined the furniture with fresh polish. Lightbulbs beamed soft color from our ceilings as though the house were staged for a quick sale. We felt like honored guests just checked in for a luxury weekend. Our hearts were bursting with gratitude.

After a short visit and an update on recent events, our friends, the benevolent flower donors, attentive to Boone's noticeable fatigue, excused themselves to leave. We walked out the front door together, lingering on the landing and talking, watching Boone sweep away yellow pollen coating the gray concrete.

We heard the horn honking. Our sixteen-year-old daughter, Sara Britton, driving for only four months, was backing out of the driveway, arm out the window, waving, and smiling.

"Bye, daddy!" she hollered. "I'm glad you're home. Be back later."

As we were saying goodbye to one another, we could see what was about to happen but couldn't get our mouths open fast enough.

In one split second: Bang, Slam, Crush. She crashed into our friend's Isuzu: $5,100 total damage. We hadn't been home an hour.

Later that day, as I was just beginning to unpack a few things, Boone resting on the family room sofa, still shaken from the crash, our phone rang. It was my sister Deborah. Heaving sobs blasted from the receiver, her words incoherent.

At first I couldn't understand *anything* she said. After a back-and-forth conversation, I finally did. There was an accident involving her son. His longtime girlfriend had been tragically killed. My sister, understandably, was inconsolable. I was numb. I was barely able to process her news.

We no longer lived in a world separated by good and bad. I realized the simple truth: bad things do happen to good people. It happens all the time. It was happening to us.

It was my mother's birthday, April 19, and she was turning seventy-one. My birthday was the next day. The celebrations we'd planned were all canceled.

Boone retreated to our bedroom and slept throughout the night and into late morning the next day. Shortly after lunch the next day, my sister called again.

Her son, anguished by the death of his girlfriend, wanted to come and stay with me. He always felt happy around me and sought refuge. I understood his longing. I wanted refuge myself. Our car was still packed and waiting to be unloaded.

"Tell him to come," I replied.

From the first hour he arrived in our home, he wallowed downstairs, day into night, crying, never leaving his room. Boone lay in our bed upstairs most of the day, silent. I would run between them, tempting each with food, beverages, and spirit-boosting conversation. Nothing worked.

It was like living in a tomb. There was so much silence in our home, the blower from the air-conditioner vent sounded like a cannon. It became unbearable. I called my sister and asked her to pick her son up. I had lasted only two long weeks.

Always optimistic until this point in my life, I became anxious, worried, and sad, like a cheerleader to a losing team. My engine was running on fumes. There was nowhere to fill up.

CHAPTER TEN

Remembered Beauty

SEASONS CHANGED AS SPRING leapt into summer. Boone had recovered from radiation, regaining some lost weight. His hair was growing back much blonder. His angular face, still handsome, seemed broader. He smiled more.

It was May when his four brothers decided to take him on a road trip, a genealogical adventure through the Midwest where their grandparents had begun their lives many years before. Clay, one of Boone's younger brothers, thought it would be a nice break for me. As they made their plans, I began making mine.

I heard about a brain tumor symposium in Chicago. The presenters were renowned physicians from all over the world and would be discussing cutting-edge treatments, clinical trial offerings, state-of-the-art equipment, and pioneers in the fields of neurology, radiology, and oncology. Even though it was geared toward physicians and people in medical fields, I felt confident I would benefit and lobbied for admission. I bought the airline tickets, grabbed my two sisters and my good friend Georgia, and we were jet-bound.

Depressing, disheartening, discouraging, and dismal—there are not enough adjectives to describe that weekend. I sat with my three-ring notebook and a sharpened pencil, writing notes in Latin as one medical doctor after another confirmed my greatest fear. I flew home as someone else, no longer confident, hopeful, or positive. I was simply scared.

The three-month mark for Boone's follow-up MRI arrived, rattling our nerves. Thankfully, it was clean, with no recurrence. The scar running down the side of his head was still visible, his new hair slow growing in that fragile location. Even so, he looked much healthier than I could remember. *He is going to be the exception; those doctors just don't know it*, I told myself, day after day.

We celebrated June, gathering for a week at Boone's family reunion, followed by July at mine. It had been five months since his surgery, and he remained in remission. As August approached, so did our twenty-fifth wedding anniversary. We talked about wanting to do something memorable. Actually, I talked about it mostly.

Although the serene romance etched in my mind conflicted with the reality of the present, I wanted to feel joy again, if just for a weekend. We decided to go back to the place we honeymooned—Sea Island, Georgia.

The Cloister, a stunning hotel with barrel tiles, creamed stucco walls, and tropical landscaping, is the landmark of Sea Island. It was designed by famed architect Addison Mizner of Palm Beach, Florida, and completed in 1928.

My sisters and I made memories there in our youth, spending the month of July there with my mother and Mazelle. Daddy stayed behind working at his medical clinic during the week and would join us on the weekends. Fireflies danced to their glittering beat by night, and by day fluffy white clouds cushioned themselves against a brilliant blue sky. It was a magical place for me.

From sunup to sundown, activities were planned: jeep train rides along the beach, scavenger hunts, sand dollar searches, horseback riding, swimming, golf, and tennis. Families bustled about, filling the pool chairs, beach chairs, and shuffleboard court.

Delectable smells drifted through the air from the beach club where the buffet was set each day; tables were filled with chicken, egg, and tuna salad; five different tossed salads; lobster; roast beef; ham; cold cuts; warm cuts; and the usual smorgasbord of varieties. The dessert table, wrapped around the back of the same room, spilled over with cakes, pies, cookies, and more.

I learned to swim. I had my first kiss on the steps of the Cloister with a boy named Jack Portman, who later became a world-renowned architect. As a teenager, I sat in the foyer admiring the volumes of honeymooners' photo albums encased in a locked bookcase. The smiling faces had graced those halls since 1940 and were splattered across each page of the thick volumes. Presidents, Hollywood stars, and ordinary lovers adorned each page. I dreamed of honeymooning there one day, and as a lucky bride, I did. Now our photograph smiled back from those same pages.

I needed Sea Island, this place I knew to deliver peace, tranquility, and happiness. We packed our bags and left for our anniversary weekend. But the smells and sounds that once comforted me there did little to welcome me. My enthusiasm was ambushed from the moment we checked in. We changed rooms twice in the first hour because Boone's sense of smell was so sensitive to everything in the room: carpet, bedspread, mattress, pillows, drapes, and even previous occupants.

Looking at our suitcases, our room, and Boone, I realized that some things should be remembered as they were.

Over that weekend, I began to notice changes in Boone's personality. It was not apparent to anyone else, but the subtleties were there. He was edgy, tired, and less engaging in conversation.

While walking on the beach together, his comment didn't take me by surprise. "I think I should go to Houston, give that guy a try, if that next MRI shows something."

"You mean that doctor on *Dateline*?" I saw him interviewed a few weeks ago and mentioned the interview to Boone. At the time, he didn't show much interest.

"Yeah, the guy you told me about."

"Okay." I blinked away my tears.

With his arm loosely wrapped around my shoulders, we walked along the shore in quiet calm, the summer breeze chilling my raised goose bumps. Seagulls sang a mating song. I prayed it wasn't the ebb tide of our married life and our last anniversary.

CHAPTER ELEVEN

Tribe and True

FOUR DAYS AFTER OUR uncelebrated anniversary, we left Sea Island, traveling back in our quiet car with zero conversation. I drove the two hundred miles thinking about alternative treatments as Boone slept. A follow-up MRI wasn't scheduled for another three weeks, yet Boone was thinking negative thoughts, expecting a tumor recurrence. *Why?* I wondered.

We arrived home from our trip weary. I unpacked the unworn, still-folded clothes from both suitcases and made us a bite to eat. Later that day I was scrolling on the computer, twisting my finger around a patch of my unruly hair when the phone rang. The stranger asked to speak to Boone.

"Who's calling?" I quizzed.

He was vague with a funny accent, so I couldn't really understand his name. I assumed it was work related, since Boone was still trying to work part-time.

I heard Boone talking from the other room as I continued researching on the computer, barely listening to his side of the conversation.

I read late into the night and forgot to ask Boone who called until the next morning.

"Who was the guy with an accent that called?" I asked while unloading the dishwasher.

"Guy I hunt with in New Mexico."

"Why'd he call? Did he hear you weren't coming?" I kept unloading the dishwasher.

Over the last years, usually in September, Boone hunted at the Mescalero Apache Reservation in southeastern New Mexico. He and some friends paid a lot of money for the privilege to hunt some of the finest bull elk, cow elk, bear, and wild birds in North America.

Large-game hunting was Boone's passion, one I didn't care two hoots about: the camouflaged attire, guns and armor, pursuit, and the trophy-kill taxidermy. I had pretty much accepted it as something Southern men liked to do.

I also didn't know much about Boone's annual visit with the Native Americans at the reservation. I was curious about his phone call, though.

He still didn't answer as he stood gazing out the kitchen window, his back to me. When he turned around, his eyes were watering.

"I guess he heard you weren't coming this year, huh?" I sat down in the chair near him, reached out, and rubbed his leg.

"He wants me to fly out there," he whispered.

"What? You can't fly there."

"There's a special ceremony he wants to have, just for me."

"What kind of ceremony?"

"It's like a healing thing. They've never done it for anyone outside their tribe, but he wants me to come."

"Huh?"

"They want to try and heal me. It's an honor. Who knows, maybe they can."

"Yeah, I'd like to know how," I whispered under my breath.

I was the perfect audience, though, since alternative treatments, homeopathy, acupuncture, and anything remotely kin was where my loyalty still lay. I just hadn't thought of medicine men yet.

He didn't answer but stared through me. I waited. He walked past as though I were invisible, went back to our bedroom, and crawled into bed.

We were on our way to Santa Fe three days later. The decision to board the plane heading for New Mexico was not spontaneous by any means. Boone worried the healing ceremony offered by the Mescalero chief might compromise his personal religious beliefs, his spiritual faith, perhaps even his mortal soul.

He had began agonizing shortly after the phone call with the chief, pacing our family room, his shoulders hunched, and his head hanging. His silence belied his personal torment; he was clearly troubled. Yet any unsolicited guidance, suggestions, or opinions I offered were ignored. He was disengaged from any conversation with me on the subject.

By the second day, I'd had enough. I was a weary and frustrated spectator, suggesting that he seek counsel from our Episcopal priest. He agreed, called him, and they met. Whatever was said between the two of them, the struggle suffocating his conscience seemed less weighty afterward. Maybe this journey might deliver the miracle we were searching for.

The Albuquerque airport was nondescript, and we were exhausted from our predawn flight. Our edgy and nervous formality sifted with the stale airport air. We sat quietly together eating our turkey sandwiches at a crumb-covered Formica countertop in a dim-lit corner of the airport.

We were awaiting the arrival of someone from the reservation who was to meet, greet, and transport Boone. In truth, I was expecting an Indian, maybe wearing a breechcloth edged with a fringe of porcupine quill. I even wondered if he might wear a feathered headdress with tall and narrow feathers from some poor dead golden eagle. But the person who arrived was a thin, taciturn man wearing blue jeans, a khaki shirt, and cowboy boots. He didn't look like my idea of an Indian at all.

I could see from Boone's posture how unsettled and nervous he was, the sadness and concern cloaking him like a cape. I was just as anxious, wondering if I trusted this stranger. It had been six months since the surgery, and I was the only person I trusted. I was Boone's sole caregiver. It was almost unthinkable that I was relinquishing my assignment to some stranger, especially since he wore cowboy boots and not even moccasins.

I started to call out my sentiments of love to Boone but re-thought it and swallowed my words, gripped my fists into white balls, and watched as they walked out of the crowded airport terminal.

I convinced myself he would be fine. He knew the chief after all. I began executing my own plans: retrieve the luggage from the baggage claim, rent a car, and drive to our reserved hotel room, where, in two days' time, we would reunite.

It was at least a sixty-mile drive from the airport to Santa Fe, with little traffic and sparse scenery. I was alone for the first time in a long time. My charade, along with my armor of optimism, began to loosen. I mentally unclothed, allowing the permanent pep I wore to fall. The pianist Nyle Frank was playing "Till Only Love Remains" softly from the classical radio station. Before I knew it, I was pulling into the entrance of the Inn of the Anasazi. I began my game of pretend.

The hotel was beautifully decorated in southwestern style and Native American décor. The adobe walls, slate floors, hand-carved doors, and leather furniture were striking, matched in splendor by the stunning lobby, warm-glow lighting, and original artwork. The smell of burning embers from the fireplace lent an ambience of warmth and comfort. All of it combined was the final touch wrapping up my perfect weekend package.

Katherine, also known as KD, was waiting for me in Santa Fe. Her husband, David, a childhood friend of Boone's, was meeting him at the reservation. David knew Boone well and was privy to his turmoil and hesitation. He and his wife had journeyed the distance from Mobile, Alabama, for support.

KD and I shared wine and wonderful conversation on "nothing" subjects, away from the words *diagnosis*, *treatment*, *side effects*, and *prognosis*.

I spent my time sightseeing, shopping, and relaxing as though life were normal. Pretending, still pretending.

I felt like I was living the life I remembered. It felt good. I felt good. I even forgot for a moment why I was in New Mexico and found myself smiling and laughing. When I realized it, guilt engulfed me, changing my mood and my expression. It was as though a virus had tapped into my bloodstream, contaminating the joyful juice flowing through my veins and reminding me, once again, this was not my normal life and I must wake up.

Two days later I was standing in front of the hotel, my arms holding a shopping bag from the local market, when the long blue sedan drove up to the front door of the inn.

My welcoming smile, joyful greeting, and energetic reception were met by Boone's cheerless eyes. Few words were spoken. He just asked for the key, took the elevator up, dropped his bag inside the room, and crawled into the king-size bed.

I stood soberly watching him. An invisible black cloud seemed to drift from the blazing fire nestled in the corner of our room. I gazed at his black penny loafers lying at the foot of the bed. They were sprinkled and adorned with ceremonial yellow dust. He slept the remainder of the afternoon.

Later, KD and David joined us as we strolled along the Santa Fe Plaza and watched tourists bargain for silver and turquoise jewelry handmade by local artisans. David pulled me aside while KD distracted Boone.

"I think you guys should head home tomorrow, Prissy. You need to get Boone checked out," he said.

"His appointment isn't for three weeks."

"You can't wait three weeks. It needs to be tomorrow, wish it was today."

I guess David didn't need a gray plastic film clipped to a brightly lit box to confirm what he already suspected: the tumor was back. After all, he was a radiologist, and he'd just spent two nights on a reservation with his closest friend.

We flew back home the next day.

I could hear the hissing from the lights above us; their florescent glare grayed the painted walls. The smell of floor wax rose to mingle with the antiseptic cleanser used earlier to wipe down the overused patient table. My sensitive nose recognized the scent no cleanser could conceal—the smell of disease, specifically, cancer. The oncologist, Dr. Care, whom I had ruthlessly interrogated during dinner a few months earlier, walked into the examination room. He had just read the latest MRI and was shaking his head—left to right, right to left—patting Boone's arm while staring into my eyes.

"I'm sorry."

I already knew. It was as if someone had said the weather was bad as you stood in the middle of hurricane-force winds.

"Okay, what next?" I asked, watching him shake his head. "Why are you shaking your head?"

"Prissy, I'm sorry. There's nothing more. Go home. Enjoy each other."

"I don't believe that. I won't accept it. If you can't help, we're going to Houston."

Boone sat quietly, nonresponsive, seemingly not comprehending as I negotiated his very life. Dr. Care assured me the doctor in Houston would be a waste of Boone's remaining time and our money. *Did he call him a quack?*

He said if I was adamant about more treatment, there was a clinical trial at Duke University, a speck of promise, but too early to tell.

"No clinical trial," Boone whispered.

It had been seven months to the day since Dr. Mean operated, shattering our world with his grim prognosis: one year at best. Since that day, I'd wasted no time on tears, fears, or Western medical miracles. I had researched every single day for alternative anything and everything. Now we were running out of time.

Dr. Care patted Boone on both shoulders. When he turned around, I saw the tears in his eyes. He hugged and held me for a long moment then released me as he whispered, "Good luck, Prissy."

We walked down the familiar corridor toward the waiting room. I saw her sitting there, my blond-haired, blue-eyed, twenty-year-old daughter, Garrett, who insisted she make the day trip with us. As we approached, I saw the hopeful innocence radiating from her, and the composure I'd concealed for the last seven months dissolved. My deep pain churned; I felt it surfacing. I turned and ran to the nearest bathroom. I could hear Garrett calling after me.

"Mom! What's wrong with her?"

Glancing back, I watched as Boone draped his thin arm over her shoulder, pulling her close to him.

"Let her go, honey. Just let her be," I heard his hoarse voice tell her as I turned the corridor.

I found the bathroom door, not caring if it said "Men" or "Women." I slid down the wall of the stall and squatted on the floor. My anguished sounds mimicked a wounded animal.

A few minutes later, I pulled myself up, blew my snotty nose, and walked to the sink. *Am I having a breakdown?* I splashed my face with cold water and stared at my aged reflection in the mirror.

If this was combat and Boone was a critically wounded soldier, what would I do? Was I someone who would just leave him on the field, bleeding, to die? Or would I try to carry him on my back and scream for a medic? I knew my answer. I began to compose myself and walked out the bathroom door. The war was not over—not yet anyway.

CHAPTER TWELVE

Hope Springs Forth

WE LEFT THE CANCER center and forgot about lunch, our customary ritual after follow-up appointments. Boone didn't say a word to either of us, just climbed in the backseat and lay down. I remembered how Garrett's inner voice urged her to transfer to Florida State over Christmas break. Her decision had been an unrecognizable gift at that time. As she drove the three of us back home, with broken, overburdened hearts, I finally understood how fortuitous her decision was. She and I never stopped crying, while Boone slept the whole way.

When we arrived back home, I brought up the idea of the Houston guy—the one I'd seen on *Dateline*, the one I'd been researching, the one we'd talked about on the shoreline at Sea Island. Boone stared, listened, but was uninterested in making decisions. His enthusiasm was gone. After Dr. Care told him there was no hope, everything changed for Boone. He was completely different. What fight he had left had faded. Not mine, though. I hadn't, couldn't, or wouldn't accept the opinion of his oncologist, no matter his credentials, no matter his caring way.

Boone was ensconced in his own personal hell, infused with overwhelming sadness and an almost catatonic fear of the inevitable. My authoritative, logical, and intelligent husband, the man I had shared decisions with all my adult life, had departed. I was left to figure it all out alone. It was an overwhelming responsibility.

Hour after hour, night after night, as Boone slept fitfully and alone in our bed, I continued searching. I was afraid to relax the momentum I'd built during his first weeks of treatment, afraid I would somehow lose ground, along with any sliver of hope. It was still clinging like a fading shadow.

"Please stop, Prissy. Come to bed. Lie down with me," he asked one night as I squinted at the computer. It was around eight o'clock, still light outside.

"Later, I'll be there later. It's too early."

"Please."

"Boone, I will. Later, okay?" It was a simple request, and I responded with a thoughtless, distracted answer. How could I spend hours curled up sleeping when I was the only one who could find someone to save him? I had no time to comfort him. Maybe later I would, but not yet.

When later came, I slid under the covers and warm sheets. I inhaled the soothing scent of the freshly laundered pillowcases and rolled closer to him. The smell of his cotton T-shirt mingled with the scent of Ivory soap still lingering in his pores from an earlier shower. It was wonderful yet unbearable.

I listened to his breathing and quiet moans. *Are they nightmares?* I wondered. *How can he sleep with a sentence of death? Is this the mercy of brain disease?* I stared and prayed into the silent, still, and darkened room until my same worn prayers pulled me into sleep. I slept worriedly for only a brief time.

In the next few days, I selected, eliminated, and finalized all my researched choices. I kept coming back to the same one, over and over. I turned my notebook to a new sheet of paper, grabbed my pen, and started writing and underlining unfamiliar words to look up later. I fixated on certain words: *nontoxic, naturally occurring, organic, few side effects.* I remembered the scam of the purple slush foot solution, wondering if this was different.

I called him Dr. Hope, though his real name was Stanislaw Burzynski, MD. He was born in Poland, where he trained as a biochemist and physician. To some, he was known as the "doctor of last resort." He had been prosecuted in our courtrooms for years and was considered one of the most controversial alternative doctors in the country.

It all began in the early 1970s, when he discovered that people with cancer lacked a certain peptide in their blood and urine, while those who were cancer-free had a plentiful supply.

As a biochemist, he invented an alternative cancer drug therapy he called antineoplastons. He believed and claimed these were nontoxic and naturally occurring peptides, amino acid derivatives, and organic acids that fought cancer with few side effects, causing no harm to healthy cells.

It's not entirely clear how these antineoplastons work, but it is believed they act as biochemical microswitches, turning off the genes called oncogenes and activating genes called tumor-suppressor genes, which fight cancer. Since they are harmless to the healthy cells, antineoplastons can flood the bloodstream, targeting only the cancer cells. The word that resonated with me was *nontoxic*, and I was still clinging to the word *cure*.

Dr. Hope had great success, especially with brain tumors, but because his treatment was not yet approved by the Food and Drug Administration (FDA), it was not considered a documented clinical trial, and the FDA wanted him shut down for noncompliance.

The US federal government spent years suppressing this cancer treatment, spending millions of US taxpayer dollars trying to put this pioneer scientist and inventor in jail, strip away his medical license, sabotage his trials, steal his patent, harass him, and bury him in bureaucratic regulations. He was indicted for fraud and seventy-five counts of violating laws; some of these events were taking place right at the time we needed him. Boone was worsening. More than one smart friend, along with our daughters, encouraged me to follow my heart and fly out for a consultation. I had followed up with everyone I could think of, even those who might discourage me, namely, a friend who was a malpractice attorney. His reply surprised me: "I'd go if it were me."

Dr. Hope was featured on multiple talk shows, as well as a special edition of *Dateline*, a syndicated news show. Despite all the controversy surrounding him, I believed he was probably our last-ditch chance for remission, so I began collecting all of Boone's medical reports, X-ray films, and medical history and filling out endless hours of paperwork. Two days before our scheduled departure, our appointment was postponed; the Burzynski Clinic in Houston was shut down once again. There were more FDA charges, indictments, and a media blitz. I knew it would be resolved in a few days, though, and kept our plans. Just as I'd hoped, it was resolved, and we packed and loaded our bags for Texas.

We drove to Pensacola to take the direct flight, completely unaware of what awaited us. All I really knew was Dr. Hope believed he had a cure for cancer and the FDA wanted to shut him down. I always cheered for the underdog, so he had my vote.

We arrived in Houston the day before our scheduled appointment and picked up our rental car at the airport. The previous week, I had called and secured a room at an extended-stay motel: two bedrooms, two bathrooms, a sitting area, and a plateless and potless kitchen with an ugly dinette table.

The chain motel I chose was recommended through the Burzynski Clinic's website as clean, close-by, and family-oriented. True, it was all of the aforementioned, but the room was void of any primary colors. A bland, institutional decorator must have been color-blind and decided to just go beige. I was sitting on the uncomfortable, spring-sprung couch, staring into the space between me and the dated television, when I realized I was hungry.

I couldn't remember when I had last eaten. I was struggling to maintain my weight, had noticed the bagginess of my slacks and sweaters during the last weeks, and knew another five pounds had slipped away. I needed to stock the kitchen with groceries, so I decided to find a store. I checked on Boone, saw he was fast asleep, and decided not to wake him. I left a note next to his pillow telling him I would be right back.

In the lobby standing behind the front desk, a young boy repeated the directions to me twice. I was confident I understood and knew where I was going. But one wrong turn was all it took: the flyover, beltway, and hell-way were in front of me within five minutes. I had no idea where I was, where I was going, or how to get back. I could think of nothing but Boone waking up and looking around with no idea where I went, or worse, where he was.

There was one flyover after another, with no exits anywhere in sight. Each road sign was above me before I could read it. I began to panic, tried to calm myself with deep breathing and meditation chants, but continued feeling sweaty and light-headed, like I might faint.

I told myself to relax, loosened my white-knuckled grip on the wheel, and accelerated my speed. I was going between twenty and forty miles per hour while everyone else sped past at seventy to eighty miles per hour. When I finally saw an exit, I pulled off and found myself in a run-down neighborhood. I began searching for a safe place to ask for directions when there it was: a shiny black car decorated with gold lines and bejeweled with the glassed light. I felt like Dorothy in *The Wizard of Oz* at the end of her yellow brick road. The patrolman was talking to the clerk inside the minute-market, turning his head slightly and glancing my way as I walked through the smeared glass door. I planted myself in front of him and began blubbering.

"Are you okay, ma'am?" he asked, probably fearing I'd been assaulted or robbed.

That poor man—I told him everything, way more than he wanted to hear. I went on and on, from the beginning of Boone's diagnosis to the present, and how I got lost. All he wanted was a cup of coffee; instead, he got me and an hour of sobbing from what seemed like a lunatic woman sprung from *The Jerry Springer Show*. When he thought I was composed enough, he told me how to get back to the hotel, but before he could finish, I started crying again. I didn't know if he felt sorry for me, thought I was crazy (probably), or was just nice. At any rate, he escorted me through the noodle-nest freeway and back to the motel—forty miles—where I found Boone still fast asleep. It was only our first day.

The next day I awoke with newfound optimism, trying to ooze some of my cheer toward Boone. I knew he was scared, but I continued to play it down. Always the cheerleader, I would have better served him as his coach. Then I might know how to encourage him with the spirit of fighting, winning, and never giving up.

I waited for him in our small living room as he brushed his teeth in a slower than usual routine. By nine o'clock, we were in the car and on our way.

Pushing through the double doors and into the waiting room of the facility, nothing could have prepared me for what I saw. It was as though I stood in the middle of a refugee camp in a third-world country where starvation prevailed in epidemic proportions.

There were four overworn dark-brown couches and more than a dozen metal chairs. The most gravely ill were half lying, half sitting, their blank stares and gaunt faces pasty, a fusion of yellow and dull gray.

It looked something like Dante's *Inferno*, where the sign read, "Abandon all hope, ye who enter here." Yet here, the sign would read, "Last Hope Landing—Welcome All."

I looked around the room, from one couch to the next, from one chair to another. It was a smorgasbord of sufferers: infants and children, men and women, some speaking foreign languages. Everyone looked related, their resemblance in pallor and posture almost exact, with dazed, bloodshot eyes defining their despair. They wore that weariness from long journeys like issued uniforms.

As we walked through the maze of people, we located two seats in the far corner of the room and slid down onto them in silence, lost in our personal space, somewhere between hope and hell, and waited for Boone's name to be called.

I watched a young girl with bony shoulders. Her bald head was glowing from the beaming florescent lights above her. The fresh nine-inch scar across her scalp was still visible as she burrowed her head in her mother's neck. The mother draped a comforting arm around her and rubbed her limp arm.

Across the room, I heard a sick and hungry baby crying. Next to him, a dark-haired boy with umber eyes whined in a hoarse whisper, his mother soothing and stroking his back. A few months earlier, she might have scolded him for whining.

Those suffering diverged from those not, as the nots streamed through their own lives, unaware of their vast fortune: good health. It was the one thing money couldn't buy—or could it? Inside my black patent leather wallet was an American Express card with a name etched in gold waiting for my $10,000 swipe. I had borrowed it from one of Boone's law partners, Fred, a life-saving friend.

Another hour went by before Boone's name was finally called. The nurse led us down the hall. I struggled to maneuver the large manila envelope housing the latest brain images as I carried my oversized purse and the cumbersome briefcase stuffed with copies of medical records. I was wavering between anxious anticipation and dread: we were going to meet with someone who was both a renowned scientist and a charged-but-not-yet-convicted criminal.

I had rehearsed my argument for Boone's acceptance into this international, exclusive, and unorthodox program as I wondered how each patient was selected in this circle of the chosen few. I knew Boone could be rejected. I had analyzed every reason they might give and had an answer ready.

We walked into the small office. It was nothing like I'd imagined. Credentials hung unevenly in unmatched frames on the walls. The desk was large, plain brown, and piled high with papers in various stacks, making the occupant, Dr. Hope, look small as he peered up from his sturdy leather chair.

In the somber room, sun streaked through the barely cracked blinds, making stripes of light on the drab-colored walls. This man, the renowned Dr. Stanley Burzynski, was wearing a pressed blue shirt with a beige tie and no jacket. The images I remembered seeing on television of him only a few days before contradicted what I saw today. He looked kinder, although a little unhealthy to me, perhaps resulting from his latest FDA conflict and courtroom drama. The nurse escorting us made the introductions then closed the door as she left.

We sat in silence as this ordinary-looking man, who was believed to have an extraordinary mind, reviewed Boone's film and latest medical summary. We waited for him to speak. When he finally did, his English was broken and bore a heavy accent. He began telling us about his program, its success, and the cancers he found to be the most treatable. I was listening, trying to interpret his words, but also watching Boone's reaction, wondering if he understood anything Dr. Hope was saying. I was having trouble myself.

"I am not sure I can help; I am afraid not."

Whew. I understood those words, broken English and all. When I'm nervous, I can't stop talking, and I was nervous. I began delivering the rehearsed plea in my best Southern vernacular, jabbering to the back of Dr. Hope's head as he studied the film image of Boone's brain clipped to the florescent box on the wall behind his messy desk. I stopped only when his chair swirled back around, startling me.

"Okay, we will try, but it is not good. There will be no guarantee, you understand?"

Everything he said after that was in fast-forward as I struggled to understand and comprehend: the contract, signatures, protocol, preparations, treatment, daily regimen, our financial responsibility, my responsibility, Boone's responsibility, the clinic's responsibility. When I heard the words *hospital* and *chest port*, I stopped him. *Had I missed something? Exactly how was this treatment performed? Why had I not read that anywhere in my months of research?*

"I'm sorry. What did you say?" I asked.

"We will schedule his outpatient procedure, the chest port, at the specialty hospital for tomorrow."

I saw the color drain from Boone's face and knew it was over. Since his cranial surgery, he had developed an overwhelming fear of hospitals, resulting in the need for me to locate off-site facilities that would perform each six-week-interval MRI ordered by his oncologist and required by our insurance company. It was not just fear but an absolute refusal on his part. It was a constant challenge for me.

"Is there another way to administer the drug, aside from the port?" I asked, my eyes darting from Dr. Hope to Boone and back again. "You see, he won't go to a hospital."

Boone sat mute, shaking his head left and right.

"I'm afraid not," Dr. Hope said. "Normally we might be able to administer an oral dosage. Not in his case. Too late. Not enough time for that. He must have a port."

All three of us remained silent for a moment. A migraine was beating its way into my head.

"But there is an off-site facility we use sometimes." He pulled his glasses off and leaned forward on his desk toward me and continued. "It is not part of our associated hospital, but a few patients have gone there in the past. If you like, I will make arrangements." I watched his eyebrows arch higher up his forehead, wondering if this was a statement or a question.

I looked at Boone. He was white as a ghost.

"Okay, that'll work," I replied after a one-second pause.

I handed him the borrowed credit card, along with the stack of signed papers bearing Boone's illegible signature scribbled on the bottom of every unread page. I no longer cared what was signed. He had been accepted into the program, and we were registered for hope.

We left the clinic with prescriptive orders to go directly to the other facility for Boone's chest port. The specialty hospital they favored and recommended was close to where I'd parked our car. We could have walked to it, but no amount of coercion would convince Boone to go there. He saw the word *hospital.* We would have to go to the other place only a few of Dr. B's patients had gone to, a place he called a clinic.

"I'm tired," Boone whispered so quietly I wasn't sure I heard him. "Take me back."

"Let's walk over there and get your port. We can be in and out of there and have it done in no time, honey. It'll be okay. They do it all the time," I said.

"No. Take me back."

We drove back to our hotel. I'd forgotten I had reinforcement coming to town and felt relieved when I remembered. Boone's oldest brother, Dick, was flying in from San Francisco for an overnight visit. I was confident the two of us might be able to persuade Boone to get the port at the recommended hospital. We came up short, but at least Boone agreed to go to the clinic.

Late that afternoon, I was behind the wheel of our rented blue Chrysler Concorde with Dick in the backseat and Boone in the passenger seat. Before cranking the ignition, I read the scribbled directions several times, trying to figure out where we were going and not wanting a repeat of my Jerry Springer event the day before.

I headed for Harrisburg Boulevard, somewhere near Magnolia Park and the second ward on the east end of Houston. My directions were sketchy but not as sketchy as the neighborhood we were approaching. Graffiti covered not just the sidewalks but also the vacant buildings and abandoned cars lining the streets.

Nervous, I looked at everything around me and began to devise some sort of explanation for this neighborhood as Boone and Dick sat speechless and pale, both securing all the door locks. My annoying trait of excessive talking began.

"You know what I think? Some of the best doctors have the worst offices. They don't have time to spend money on fancy décor. They're far too busy serving their patients, putting their money into technology and seminars. You know, my favorite doctor in Tallahassee has a really run-down office, but he is the best surgeon I know."

I took a breath as I looked around at the seedy neighborhood and the dilapidated buildings, wondering what the hell we were doing here. When we found the address, all three of us sat in silence, but not for long. I jumped out of the car. "Let's go."

Inside, the waiting room was everything it wasn't supposed be: filthy, run-down, and unattended by any front desk employee. I found a small, dented bell at a self-serve counter and rang it. A Hispanic man walked out wearing blue scrubs. He had dazed eyes and a chin of scruffy hair.

"*Les puedo ayudar?*" he asked, half-asleep.

"What did he say?" I looked toward Dick.

He translated for me. The man was asking if he could help us.

"We were sent here by the Burzynski Clinic staff . . . um . . . for a chest port?" I said as a half question and half statement. *Did I really say that standing in this Godforsaken place? Are we mad?*

"*Oh sí. Vengan a la puerta posterior y les puedo ayudar.*"

I received another translation from Dick: "Oh yeah, come on back and I can take care of that."

Did he just say "take care of that"? I wondered, alarmed and grabbing Boone's arm. "Get up, let's go."

I left Dick completely dumbfounded, speechless, and well, shell-shocked, as I took his younger brother's hand and led him back through the squalid hall.

We walked into what could be described only as a mock operating room. It was the wrong color and had no antiseptic smell, no bright lights, and worse, no staff wearing sterile coveralls, booties, and masks. The scruffy-bearded man asked Boone to lie down on the table, which he did, probably since he was too scared to argue. I was told to sit on the far side of the room where I found a wounded chair, its third leg damaged. I heard him ask Boone if he was ready, but I was too shaken to even open my mouth.

Fifteen minutes later the procedure was over. Boone's face was a mask of fright, his fingers touching the plastic tube taped across his chest as he lay on the morgue-gray operating table. Everything was foreign: the object attached to Boone, the unshaven Hispanic doctor, the back-alley facility, and worst of all, me. I no longer recognized this stranger who had moved within my own skin, goading me toward everything unfamiliar with new and fearless fury.

CHAPTER THIRTEEN

Not a Cliché

IT WAS OUR THIRD morning in Houston, the day after meeting Dr. Hope and getting Boone's port. I rolled over in our hotel bed and struggled to open my eyes and read the digital alarm clock. I could see the red line wiggling on the screen of the small clock. I thought it looked like a five but my eyes weren't yet focused. The numbers 5:45 finally became clearer as I stretched my toes toward the foot of the bed and tapped my outstretched fingers on the headboard, peering at the numbers again with only one eye. I lay there a few minutes longer, calculating what the time was at home: only 6:45 a.m. in Tallahassee—much too early to call anyone. I looked and saw Boone still fast asleep.

Craving some coffee and wearing a pair of Boone's socks and his oversized T-shirt, I slid off the hard hotel mattress and shuffled to the meagerly supplied kitchen. It reminded me of some kitchen I'd seen in a movie once.

I busied myself measuring the bottled water, pouring it into the well of the ancient coffee pot, scooping two extra tablespoons from the Folgers can into the filter. Finally, I pushed the red button and leaned on the counter, watching and waiting for the first drip, a tired yawn pulling my face.

The aroma began percolating around me, catering to at least one of my deprived senses—smell. I knew very soon one more sense might be gratified—taste. The coffee was the only normal thing right now. I was afraid Boone might wake up and ask me to pour it out, the smell making him nauseated. He was never a coffee drinker and couldn't understand my ritual of perking, pouring, and sipping.

I reflected on our previous day's excursion and realized Boone might still be upset from the trip down graffiti row, the dingy and dark medical facility, and worse, that port with the plastic attachment now hanging from his chest. It had been just as hard for Dick to swallow when we left the clinic, the evidence apparent to me by his demeanor as we drove to the airport for his departing flight.

In less than two hours, we were to report to the clinic. I went back to the bedroom to wake up Boone, barely finishing my coffee.

I guess I assumed we would arrive at the clinic and they would escort Boone back for the first of his magic treatments as I sat in the waiting room reading a novel or visiting with other caregivers. That was our routine at the cancer center during the six weeks of grueling radiation four months earlier. So when a nurse wearing lipstick traveling far outside her lips called both our names, I was puzzled.

"You want me to come back too?" I asked her.

She looked at me as though I were drunk. "Yes, I do," she said curtly.

We got up and followed her through the door.

I counted fourteen green recliners in the large room where she led us. Boone was asked to sit in one of the few remaining empty ones as I stood by. He was nodding his head up and down, responding to some questions the nurse asked. She leaned over and pulled a lever to recline the chair, and his feet immediately shot into the air. Next to his chair was an IV bag hanging from a pole. The nurse hooked it up to the rubber tubing dangling from his chest port that peeped through his open-buttoned shirt then offered him a blanket, though I was the one shivering.

I was looking around for a chair for myself, still unsure why I was in this back room and not in the waiting room. *Where am I supposed to sit?* I wondered. As my eyes flitted around the room, I spotted two large conference tables with seven to ten chairs around each one. I could see positioned on the table in front of each chair the following items: plastic tubing, a bottle of rubbing alcohol, a pamphlet, a clipboard with notepaper and a pen, two IV bags, a urinal container, a plastic measuring cup, cotton squares, and a fanny pack. Oh yeah, and a bottle of water. In front of the two conference tables stood a large chalkboard; on it were neatly drawn diagrams beside a long numbered list. Several large boxes were stacked on each side of the chalkboard.

Those of us who arrived with sick loved ones were told to take a seat, and the orientation began. An articulate and professional nurse stood before fourteen strangers, most of us with nothing in common, yet each of us with everything in common: a dying loved one sitting in one of those recliners being infused with $10,000 of liquid gold.

The nurse began by expressing her sympathy, support, and understanding. Her next breath explained our responsibility, our challenges, and the demands we must face, along with the requirements to know what we were doing and how we were doing it. As I recall, it went something like this:

"For the next two weeks, you will be trained by a staff member here at the Burzynski Clinic on becoming the equivalent of an intensive care nurse. You will be responsible for readying the IV bags for use, administering proper dosage, measuring the input and output of all liquids ingested and excreted during each twenty-four-hour period, then charting these measurements for our review the next day.

"Beginning today, you will be taught how to prime IV bags, flush chest tubes, clean the ports, and sanitize your surroundings. You will be responsible for all these procedures, starting tonight when you leave our clinic. We are only here to train you, so please understand after these few weeks you will return home and must be able to provide these treatments to your patient.

One more thing: before the patient is discharged from our care, protocol requires the patient have a final MRI. This will be performed the day of discharge. Now, do you have any questions, and are we ready to get started?"

We? What is this "we" shit? Nowhere in any of their literature had I read I would be administering treatment. I was dumbfounded. I thought of jumping up and snatching out Boone's IV and retrieving him from this nightmare right that minute, I really did. But they had my money—paid in advance. Well, technically, it wasn't even my money.

I didn't know who to call, what to do, or where to turn. If I tried to prioritize the worst events up to that point since the day Boone was diagnosed, this was number one.

It was as though they were shoving me into surgery and ordering me to operate without ever teaching me anatomy. Yet it was obvious this was not elective participation. They were not asking me if I would do this but telling me I was going to. That cliché "desperate times call for desperate measures" was valid, but desperate times were happening to us over and over again. My trying to keep up a façade of pep, positivity, and faith—despite unanswered prayers—had worn me down.

I tried to be brave, optimistic, and the cheerleader I had always been. I was so scared, but I decided then I had to do it, I could do it, and I would do it. I would save Boone. I knew I needed to circle, paw, and chew my newest bone. After all, it was the one I wanted most.

CHAPTER FOURTEEN

Sign of Resolution

ONLY TWENTY MINUTES AFTER the instruction from Nurse Ratched, our newest routine began inside the walls of the clinic in Houston, Texas. From that morning and every morning thereafter while in Houston, we would arrive at the clinic by eight o'clock. Boone would be housed in his recliner, and I would settle in my conference chair and start kneading IV bags, one after another, making sure not one air bubble remained. When I finished one, another would be retrieved from the big box. I would keep going, stopping only for a pee or a stretch.

Each day a compassionate and patient nurse would review my previous night's chart to see if the twenty-four-hour input of antineoplastic drip and the output of urine were in the range of the actuated numbers. The indignity I felt as I collected those numbers grew worse as days went by.

The people sitting next to me, once strangers, became friends. Together we massaged bubbles from bags and talked about sick husbands, wives, children, and parents, everyone exhausted but no one complaining.

Like in most cities, the arsenic hours for traffic in Houston were eight in the morning and five in the evening, the very hours of our scheduled travel commute. I wouldn't drive from that clinic to the hotel until traffic hour was over or lessened, so we went around the block to the movie theater to see whatever was playing. When the movie was over, we would go to a restaurant for dinner where neither one of us ate or talked. Finally, we'd travel back to the hotel, drained of energy, conversation, and optimism.

I used the hotel's Formica dining table and set it up with the same supplies and configuration as the clinic, along with prescribed pharmaceuticals, their names unknown. I would sit at the table and ready the bags for that night's dosage as Boone wandered in silence around me and our lackluster surroundings. With little food in our room and neither one of us with appetites, we both ate little, becoming thin and unhealthy looking.

Boone's brother Clay kept us company on his days off as an airline pilot. He would join us at the clinic, restaurant, or movie.

After three long weeks, November approached, and so did Boone's upcoming birthday. I worried we'd be alone. Clay and his wife, Sherry, lived a short distance from Houston and invited us to their home for dinner, cake, and ice cream, offering to pick us up and take us back to the hotel, which was a plus for me, since I was still terrified of the Houston transportation system.

I was so excited to be leaving that depressing clinic and our dreadful hotel room you would have thought I was invited to a Texas gala. But it was not as I hoped. Boone crawled into their bed and slept through dinner, his cake, and the entire celebration. Clay and Sherry tried to make conversation, later settling for awkward silence.

A few days afterward, I came up with an idea that might boost our spirits—fly the girls to Houston and surprise Boone as a belated birthday gift. They had been calling every single day, begging to come. Every time we talked, they asked how he was, and I would put on my big-girl pants and make something up.

"Daddy is doing great. I think the treatment is working, I really do."

"Can we come out, Mom? Please?"

"Not yet. Later you can. He's at the clinic all day, dog tired when we get back to the hotel. There would be nothing for you guys to do all day." I was the mother still wanting to protect her children.

Excuse after excuse I gave, but he just didn't want them to come. I didn't know why. Regardless, the isolation became unbearable for me. I believed they might lift his spirits and made airline reservations anyway.

When they walked into the hotel room, it did not go as I hoped. It was horrible. Boone was angry, *really* angry, at me and both girls.

"What are you doing here? I told you not to come. I don't want you here," he shouted to them.

I was livid. They were crying. I was crying. He was crying. Only much later would I understand his reasoning: these were his babies. He still had his pride and didn't want them to see him like this. They stayed the night and flew home the next day, more grown up than when they'd arrived only thirty hours earlier.

The following morning the weather was beautiful. As we drove to the clinic, I apologized for the girls' visit and told Boone I understood his reaction. He was drifting further and further away from any communication with me. I attempted to make small talk.

"What a glorious day." There was a crisp November breeze gently brushing the fall palette of leaves. "Look at that gorgeous sky, would you? God has painted a perfect portrait today, I'm telling you. Those ribbons of white streaming through look like script. It could be a message for us—see if you can read it."

He didn't answer.

"Please. You need to be thankful, you know. Here we are driving to a place that is helping you. Why can't you appreciate it?"

No answer.

I pulled into the parking lot, put the car in park, and was halfway out of the car. He pulled my arm, pulling me back inside.

"It's easy for you to see blue sky, white clouds, be thankful. You're living. I'm dying. There is nothing to be thankful for.

Don't you get that? Try seeing it from where I sit." He turned his head from me and stared ahead through the windshield.

I cried for a minute or so. I pulled myself together when I saw the person in the car next to us watching.

"If you die, I've got no life. Don't you get that?" I mumbled between wiping tears and snot. "You are my life. I can't conceive me . . . without you."

He reached over for my right hand and rubbed it in both his hands. "You'll go on, Prissy. You will. You'll have a happy life. I know you. I want you to, I do. It's just hard."

We both cried under God's perfect sky.

I recall it to be the last real conversation we ever had.

The next day, another brother, Kris, offered to fly out from Marathon, Florida. I believed the birthday saga, along with the children's nightmarish visit, had been transmitted by telephone wire between family members. Someone had summoned him.

Since we had a two-bedroom, two-bath suite, I suggested he stay with us, hoping he could solicit some conversation from Boone. The silence was maddening by then. After the visit and early dinner, the weariness of the journey tired Kris. He went to bed, and so did we.

Early the next morning, I found Kris kneeling on the floor next to his bed in the same clothes as the day before, looking worn and pale. He'd pulled his back and had been there all night in that same position. He didn't have the heart to call out for me.

"I came to help, not hinder," he explained.

It didn't really matter by then. Boone had given up, was sick of it all: the clinic, the apartment, the port, the fanny pack he wore twenty-four hours a day housing his IV bag, the urinal I pushed against him every time he peed, the steroid drugs, and the mandatory MRI ordered weekly to see if any of this was working.

"We aren't quitting. You're not giving up," I lectured Boone as Kris sat on the couch, looking pained, sad, and helpless. "You need to think positive, that's all. Why can't you do that just once?" I ran into the bathroom, slammed the door, and drew a bath. Crying, I sat on the tub's ledge as the hot water steamed the room.

Later, in the bathtub, with the curtain drawn and the vent fan running, I talked to God, not quietly in silent prayers the way I had in previous months but out loud. It was as though He was sitting on the ledge next to me. I was talking into an empty space, pretending He was right there.

"Please, God, help me know what to do. Let me know if I'm wrong or making a mistake. I don't know anymore. Guide me, won't you, please? Just give me some sign, any sign, so I will know. I will do whatever you planned, whatever you want. I just need to know what that is somehow."

An hour later, I walked back into the living room to change the IV bag and dispense more medicine. Boone was standing there—*naked*. He dropped to his knees with his hands clasped in prayer and begged me to take him home. I grabbed a blanket, knelt beside him, and wrapped the blanket and my arms around him. I kissed his forehead, his cheek, then his lips and whispered over and over into his ear. "Okay, honey. I will take you home."

God had sent his message. We left Houston, along with all my hope, the very next day.

PART TWO

For a caterpillar to become a butterfly, it must change.
—*Unknown*

CHAPTER FIFTEEN

Keep On Keeping On

OUR PLANE SKIDDED AND landed roughly on the paved runway of the Pensacola airport. I began collecting our things. Despite the direct flight from Houston and the absence of young children who tire the most seasoned traveler, I had worried during the entire flight, about Boone's prognosis, our two girls, the future, and life in general. A sense of dread was lodged in the pit of my stomach. I felt alone, though Boone sat beside me. I was wondering if our car, left in the long-term parking lot more than a month ago, would start. I was unrecognizable, clothed in yesterday's wrinkled and stained warm-up suit, my hair unwashed for four days.

In single file we exited the narrow aisle of the plane. Boone was following close behind. I reached back and found his hand and clasped my fingers around his, wanting him to feel safe. The noisy terminal felt electric and looked foreign and unfriendly. Making our way to the baggage claim, I flagged a baggage handler and asked for his help, pointing to the large boxes, along with our luggage. The boxes were invaluable, full of the liquid hope I was transporting. The luggage was a necessity, nothing more.

As the baggage handler secured a cart for our belongings, Boone suggested he should get the car. His offer sounded normal; he always got the car when we traveled by plane.

Distracted with the boxes, I reluctantly agreed, reminding him where we left it. I retrieved the crumbled ticket from my purse and handed it to him. I reconsidered my decision, but he had already walked away.

Standing on the curb and looking down, I began rummaging through my wallet for dollar bills, wanting to generously tip the acne-faced, lanky handler for his arduous work.

"Get a load of that guy. What the hell is he doing?" he said to no one in particular.

I looked up and saw the large black Suburban speeding around the long-term parking lot in a bizarre way, zigzagging and circling cars and people, plowing down the chain-link fence and landscaped flower beds in its path and heading directly toward us, off the road, and onto the sidewalk.

My heart sunk. My stomach tumbled. It was Boone. He was lost, trying to find his way back to me.

Fortunately, there were no serious collisions and nothing I wasn't able to talk our way out of with airport officials. The greatest blessing was that no one was injured. I left my name and number, along with a copy of my insurance card for any damage claims.

As we drove back to Tallahassee, Boone slept in the passenger seat beside me. What a relief to be traveling on I-10 with no flyovers or snarly traffic. We were finally headed home. I should have been relieved, excited, and grateful, but instead I was disappointed, frustrated, and angry. I believed Boone hadn't given the treatment enough time to work. He had given up, and I had given in.

The message beamed down only a day earlier was clear: Go home. I prayed, and God answered with His unmistakable presence. I wondered—did He mean abandon my belief in His miracles and give up trying, or did He mean just go home?

Like the famed heroine Scarlett O'Hara in *Gone With the Wind*, I decided to worry about it tomorrow and brought home the supply of my hope medication.

It was ten thirty when we got home that November night, with no one waiting to greet us this time. I told our girls I would call once we arrived.

Boone was groggy, still half-asleep as I pulled into the dark carport. It was raining and had been for hours. Puddles of water glistened against the black tar driveway, and an abandoned hose lay curled in the flower bed. I wondered if I had left it there over a month ago or if the girls had been washing their cars.

Before unloading the luggage and boxes, I guided Boone up the stairs to the bedroom and helped him change into his pajamas, feeling more motherly than wifely. I turned off the light and listened to him moan as he slid under the plush down comforter, wondering if he even knew where he was.

The flight and parking lot escapade, along with the long car ride, had taken its toll on both of us. I looked forward to a relaxing bath, so I turned on the tub faucet, scooped in some Epsom salts, and decided to make a cup of tea while the tub filled.

As I walked from the bedroom toward the kitchen, I started to slide, catching myself on the wall before I fell. *What the hell?*

I turned on the foyer light and could not believe my eyes. The ceiling was soaked with puckering plaster leaking in huge puddles all over the hardwood floor. Not a one-bucket catch, but more like a dozen buckets. It was a Sunday night, and I was frantically thinking whom I could call. Alex was the first who came to mind, the same friend I called the day Boone forgot who I was.

The water gushed from the leak as the pouring rain blanketed the outside of the house. Meanwhile, I had forgotten I'd started the water for my nice hot bath. It ran over the ledge and spilled onto the bathroom floor—two inches deep. On top of that, it was ice cold, since the hot water heater had burned out in our absence as well.

Sweet Alex, friend, physician, and now roofer, spent an hour that stormy night spreading plastic lining two stories in the air. Days later, I would get the estimate to replace that twenty-five-year-old roof: $25,000. I didn't want to worry

Boone, so when he heard pounding and hammering above his head a few days later, I lied to him.

"That's just the neighbor putting on his new roof. It sounds like it's on top of us, doesn't it?"

Sadly, he believed me.

I guess, in retrospect, our first night back from Houston was insignificant compared to the return months earlier when our daughter's car wreck and my nephew's tragedy awaited us. The new roof and broken water heater were minor by comparison.

Two days after returning home, I received a phone call from Houston.

"Is this Mrs. Kuersteiner?" the woman asked.

"Yes, who's calling?"

"This is Rose. I'm calling from the Burzynski Clinic. You asked us to call when your husband's imaging results were read, the one he had the day of discharge."

"Are they back?" I was waiting for the beginning of her sentence to be "I'm sorry to say . . . "

Instead, a slight inflection in her raspy voice bounced from the receiver. "Well, it looks like there is some improvement in your husband's latest reading."

"What? Are you kidding me? Are you sure? What does that mean? What now?" I stuttered my questions into the phone without even waiting for her answers.

"Well, you should continue the treatments for four more weeks and then have a repeat MRI in your city. We sent all the supplies with you when you were discharged from our facility. You have them, right?"

"Yes, yes, I do. Okay, I will. Thank you *so* much." I hung up, ran to the kitchen for a steak knife, and raced up the stairs toward the unopened boxes. I stabbed the center of the first box, peeled off the top, and pulled out one of more than a dozen IV bags. I picked the best place to set up my new in-home therapy station.

I knew God's sign was to go home, but the improved image reading must mean keep going. Prissy translation: home infusions. I was trained now. I knew I could do it alone.

I decided the guest bedroom down the hall from our master bedroom would work. The room was decorated with creamy yellow coverlets and matching pillow shams over two twin beds. A very old mahogany chest sat between two large windows hinged with plantation shutters. The contrast of butter-yellow walls and dark furniture gave the room a peaceful glow. I smiled and knew it would be a perfect place.

I opened the door to the linen closet and pulled out every white sheet I could find, covering everything in the room: beds, chest, chair, and even the pictures hanging on the walls, though I don't know why. I went into the utility room and retrieved a folded six-foot table. I scrubbed it with soap, water, and alcohol then carried it up to the bedroom where I unfolded it and set it up at the foot of the beds. I draped the last sheet over the table as extra fabric heaped in piles on the cream-colored carpet. I unpacked the supplies and lined them up in perfect order. Everything all white, not a flicker of color anywhere in the room. Less than an hour earlier, it had been a tasteful duplication of Boone's favorite Williamsburg style, but not anymore. I wasn't euphoric, but certainly optimistic and, maybe, just a tad bit manic.

I closed the door to the transformed room and went to find my patient as I carried a syringe, IV bag, urinal, and a clipboard with a fresh page waiting for the newest number I would record, just as soon as I could get Boone to take a pee.

CHAPTER SIXTEEN

Thankless Thanksgiving

I FINISHED UP MY relaxing bath, my daily ritual to feed my starved soul. I lifted the drain and pulled myself up, tucking the wrapped towel snugly across my breasts. The trace drops of lavender oil beaded my skin as rising steam fogged the room. I stepped out of the tub, grabbing the hand towel to wipe down one of the mirrors. The scented candle flicked a hypnotic glow as I stared at this stranger in the mirror, wondering who she was. *Who have I become?*

It had been a few days since receiving the good news from the Houston clinic. Even after the nurse had called encouraging the continued treatments at home, I had noticed two things: Boone was getting worse, and he was recoiling each time I came near him. I'd started to realize he was afraid of me. I hadn't administered his treatment in three days, or even flushed his port, which had begun to reveal a dreadful odor. He seemed to have unilaterally decided he wasn't having any more of it or me, period.

Phoebe, a stay-at-home mom and very good friend, arrived mornings at nine o'clock with food and her library book. She would sit as though she had nothing else in the world to do, even with her three children at home, groceries to buy, and her own household to run. Sometimes she read to Boone, even though he conversed little or none. His comprehension, conversation, and motor skills were worsening at an alarming rate.

Phoebe and I talked about Boone and the changes we both had noticed. She suggested I phone the Houston clinic and alert them, and so I called. The operator connected me to the nurse on call. She listened to my frantic summary of the previous days' events. By the end of the conversation, she managed to encourage me to continue with the treatment, no matter what Boone thought, felt, or said. Agreeing I would, but feeling unsettled, I requested she send the latest MRI films, the ones performed the day we left. The ones she claimed showed "improvement."

"The doctor in Tallahassee is requesting them," I lied. The truth—there was no doctor in Tallahassee. There was no doctor, period. There was only me.

There are perks to staying in your own city for medical treatment rather than seeking care elsewhere. But by the time I discovered them, it was too late. My diligent search did find the best medical treatment from physicians, surgeons, and hospitals, but they were hours away from our home. Herein lay our problem: we had no in-town physician treating Boone, so there was no one to call when there was a question, concern, or problem. There are not many physicians willing to become an attendee by default to another physician's patient, especially when the patient has been involved in a non-FDA-approved treatment from an indicted physician. I was in a quandary, a serious quandary. I could feel another migraine beginning as the living room grew dim.

Later, I decided I would just send the films to David, our radiologist friend in Mobile who had journeyed to New Mexico to meet Boone for the Indian ceremony. Who better to tell me what the films showed or what might be happening to Boone? I wanted the truth.

I overnighted them to David the day they came from the Burzynski Clinic. I waited for his phone call. It came far too soon.

"I'm sorry . . . "

I can't recall any other words he said. I placed the phone on the receiver, sat down at the small kitchen desk, and stared at the faces of celebrity chefs, their toothy smiles grinning from my collection of cookbooks. The Western side of medicine told me one thing; the Eastern side said another. Since Boone no longer wanted to participate on either side, I put my faith in David. The war was over. Boone wasn't the exception after all, just another casualty. It was November 25, two days before Thanksgiving.

I pulled myself up from the kitchen chair, composed myself, and went to check on Boone. He was sitting on our bed, staring into space. I went into the bathroom and turned on the shower.

"Hey there, let's get you a shower, okay?"

He ignored me.

"You haven't had a shower in days."

I pulled on his arm trying to boost him up. The shower water continued to run. Finally, I maneuvered him to the steamy room, but it was futile. He wouldn't budge and tried to push my arm away. It was as though he was afraid of the running water. I turned off the shower and decided I would fill the bathtub instead. He stared at the splashing water and turned around toward me with a panicked look. I managed to coerce him over the ledge. I stood in the water with him, stripped him down, and eased him into a sitting position. The water was only two inches deep, but his alarmed reaction forced me to pull up the drain. Only then, I realized I couldn't lift him. He was too heavy, and he didn't understand how to help me, how to push himself up. We looked like a couple of sumo wrestlers as my commands and demands for Boone to help went unanswered. My frustration turned to panic, then crying, then screaming.

Garrett heard me and ran into the bathroom. She calmed me down, and together we struggled but managed to lift him from the cold and already dry tub.

"My God, I'm glad you're here," I told her. I grabbed a towel, washcloth, and bar of soap—for yet another sponge bath—and ushered Boone toward our unmade bed. I saw the terror in Garrett's eyes but said nothing. Later, she found me in the kitchen crushing Boone's medicine and pushing them inside his ice cream.

"Mom, what are you doing?"

"He won't take his steroids. I'm hiding them in his ice cream."

"No, I mean, what are you doing? We need help. Don't you see that? We have to find someone to come help us. Dad wouldn't want me seeing him like that—naked in the bathtub. You must know he was mortified. Call someone. Do something, please." She was sobbing.

She was right. I knew she was right.

It was after six that same evening when the doorbell rang. I had called Al, a surgeon friend, and asked him to drop by. I saw the sympathy in his eyes the moment I opened the door.

The news of Boone's diagnosis months earlier had spread like wildfire in our community. His grim prognosis, especially among our medical friends, was understood, expected, and accepted. I told Al I needed a favor. I wanted him to take a look at something. We walked to the family room where Boone sat watching a muted television. He greeted Boone and patted his shoulder after a failed handshake. Boone didn't recognize Al. I could tell and so could he.

I pulled up Boone's T-shirt and showed him the chest port as Boone stared at us, seemingly confused.

"I want you to remove this thing. Would you mind? He's not using it anymore. It's pretty nasty."

"What's that for, Prissy?" Al looked surprised, clearly aware chemotherapy wasn't recommended for Boone's type of brain tumor.

I told him about the treatment in Houston and Boone's clinical trial. "Here, I'll show you."

He followed me down the hall to the draped room where I had all the supplies.

I turned to say something to him. The absurdity of the sterile-looking room, as seen through the eyes of this surgeon, never occurred to me.

He gawked at the room and stood before me, stunned. "What in the world?"

I didn't know if it was a statement or a question. Studying his face, I knew not to try explaining. He would never understand.

"I'm not using any of this anymore. The port is useless. It needs to come out. Can you do that for me, for Boone?"

"Sure. Let's take him to the hospital. I'll take it out there."

"Can't you take it out here, right now? He won't go to a hospital, any hospital."

"Here? I'm not taking it out here. He needs to be under sedation."

"He won't go to the hospital."

"Explain to him it can't be done here, Prissy. I'll tell him for you."

I knew as I thanked him and closed the front door that I had to go to plan B. I picked up the phone and called Alex: friend, physician, and roofer. I told him I planned to operate on Boone; he just might want to come over.

Alex arrived within an hour of my call. A champion of nonconformity, he agreed to remove Boone's port at home. The thought of me doing it alarmed even him, my fearless friend. As an obstetrician, he had performed countless cesarean sections over the years. I knew he loved Boone like a brother and would not jeopardize his safety. Besides, he knew me well enough to know if he didn't do it, I would.

We began our preparation inside the white-draped room. Thinking we might need more help, I called my younger sister, Gina, and asked her to come over but decided to tell her why only after she arrived.

She held the 150-watt table lamp over Alex's head as he worked. I noticed the shaking of her hands before she even picked up the lamp. Her face was puke green.

We waited for Boone's sedative to take effect while Alex talked to him, explaining what he was going to do, and asked if he understood. Boone nodded his head, though I wondered if he understood anything. His worried frown seemed to soften as he relaxed and closed his eyes.

I rubbed his brow and whispered soothing words as Gina balanced the shaking lamp. In a moment's time, it was over. The entry point was sealed with a butterfly Band-Aid, the tubing discarded. The only pain inflicted was to me; I realized the port of hope was closed.

I began transitioning to the next phase in the grief process. The entry on my dance card was now acceptance, having crossed off denial, anger, negotiation, and hope.

CHAPTER SEVENTEEN

Threshold of Separation

BOONE WAS GOING TO die. He was going to live the rest of his life with us and die at home. I was trying to accept my new reality and process what it really meant. I decided I would control his death if I couldn't his life.

It was at this point that Cornelius Duhart, otherwise known as Du, moved into our home, our lives, and our hearts.

He sat beside me on my couch and held me as I cried, then he quietly waited while I composed myself. He asked questions, and I answered. I told him about the treatments I had done at home, the port removal we had performed ourselves, and Boone's refusal to bathe. I shared my everyday struggles, loneliness, sadness, and fear, all of it pouring from me as I talked to this stranger. He held my small hand in his large black hand and rubbed my knuckles with his other hand, listening to my every word.

I talked to him as I had to no one since the day Boone was diagnosed. Somehow I felt a kindred connection to this stranger, unlike I felt with anyone else. It was four days after Thanksgiving and nine months since Boone's fatal diagnosis. Thirty-eight weeks of dragging him on a treasure hunt and finding no treasures: surgery, radiation, foot soaks, medicine men, a scruffy port inserter with a Spanish tongue, an FDA-indicted physician, and—probably the worst of the lot—the barbaric treatment infused by me.

Cornelius Duhart walked into our home and into our lives when we needed him most. He came to give Boone back his dignity. In retrospect, it was the greatest gift we ever received. I was humbled. But mostly, I was tired.

I wasn't sure how Boone would respond to someone other than me caring for him. Would seeing an unfamiliar stranger—a black man, no less—around his wife and two daughters frighten him as he wondered why the man was in our house? I prepared my story, hoping Boone could comprehend and accept my white lie. Du followed me as we walked into the next room for the introduction.

"Honey, this is Cornelius Duhart. He's like our doctor, since we don't have one in town, okay?"

Boone held up his hand, his finger pointed at Du. "When you mow, make sure you bag any sticks and put them on the curb," he instructed matter-of-factly.

I was shocked, mortified, and embarrassed all at once—shocked that Boone had spoken in a complete sentence for the first time in weeks, embarrassed and mortified that he thought Du was his yardman.

Without a pause, Du said, "Yes, sir, Mr. Boone. I sure will."

I exhaled.

Du wasn't offended at all. He turned around and smiled at me. In that moment, I knew there was a rare quality inside this stranger. It was as though someone had blasted our house with oxygen. My starved, empty lungs inhaled.

"Christy, he needs to get used to me. He needs some time."

I hoped he was right, since I already knew time was our enemy.

As Du walked outside, I was about to close the front door but paused momentarily and called out, "It's Prissy, Du." I smiled. "Not Christy."

He nodded and gave me a big grin as he descended the circular staircase leading from our front porch.

We agreed Du would move in and start working the following evening, a twelve-hour night shift, seven o'clock at night to seven in the morning. He worked as a lab technician at the community hospital during the day, so this was his second job—spending nights with us, or rather, caring for Boone while I slept, something I'd done little of in the last nine months.

On his first night with us, the girls, Du, and I sat together and learned all we could about each other. Within our first hour together, it felt like visiting with a favorite girlfriend. Du was a funny man, his laugh genuine and infectious.

Garrett and Sara Britton talked about school, friends, boyfriends, poodles, and clothes. I asked about his life, family, and friends and shared stories of mine. I learned he sang in the choir, loved buying clothes, and dressed debonair on Sundays. I asked about his having so many brothers and sisters—twenty-seven. I listened as he explained.

"I be the oldest. My mamma and daddy had me, then they split up. My birth mamma left my daddy, had twenty more with another husband. My daddy got him a new wife, then they had them seven kids. That's how come there is twenty-eight of us in all, Christy."

He went on, "After a while, I moved in with my great-granddaddy. I went to live with him after my mamma and daddy split. My great-granddaddy lived to be 110 years old; he walked every single day back then. When time came where he be needing help, he wouldn't let nobody touch him but me. I took care of him 'til he died, every day, all day. I be about eighteen that time. This how I started taking care of people like Mr. Boone. It come from taking care of my great-granddaddy."

As I listened to Du's family history, I tried to comprehend how *one* woman could have twenty-one children. Even more, what in the world his great-grandfather *ate* to live to the ripe old age of 110. I also realized that Du was going to call me "Christy" no matter my name.

Afterward, we watched television for a while, all laughing at the same silliness on the series sitcom.

"Y'all go on to sleep," Du said when the clock struck ten o'clock. "We'll sleep in there." He pointed toward the guest room.

"What? Who will? You and Boone?" I asked.

"Christy, this why you hired me. I'm here, so no need for worrying. Go in your room. Get you some sleep, hear? Besides, that bed's way too high for Mr. Boone. He can't climb no more."

As Boone's legs weakened, our queen-size bed was harder for him to get in and out of. I had pulled my back a few weeks earlier helping him. In the past, our young children—and now, our small poodle—used the antique bed steps that sat nearby.

I worried about leaving Boone alone with Du, who was still a stranger to him. How could I do that? Sleeping, much less all night, sounded so good, though. It had been months since I'd slept more than three hours straight.

I gave Boone a white lie: "Sweetie, I think I've got a cold. You probably shouldn't be around me. You could catch it. You're going to sleep in the other room, okay?"

Boone had always hated sharing the bed when I had a cold, electing to sleep in our guest room. It seemed the perfect thing to tell him, and now he no longer had the verbal comprehension or composition to voice any objection. It was a chilly night, and I was crippled with exhaustion, but I still hardly slept. My blanket of guilt couldn't keep me warm.

Soon, the new routine became less intrusive. Du arrived before seven, and the three of us—Du, Boone, and I—watched television. Many nights, Garrett and Sara Britton would curl up opposite us on the matching love seat. Medical shows I previously loved were now taboo choices. We were living real medical drama; I had no interest in being entertained with some screenwriter's fictional version.

I pretended to watch whatever shows the girls and Du chose. Mostly though, I watched Boone, studied him and every move he made: his breaths, the times he blinked, the angle of his handsome face, his profile as he stared at some silliness beamed from the television. I daydreamed of first meeting him, a memory that filled me with nostalgic sadness and happiness simultaneously.

I was a junior at Florida State University. Southerners were everywhere on campus that Sunday afternoon. It was a Greek tradition called Tea Patrol. Translation: Check out girls.

Traveling at a snail's pace in their cars, a parade of boys gawked at the college girls sprinkled across the lawns of the various sorority houses. Rush had officially started. Boone was one of the gawkers. I was one of the hundreds of coeds gathering for the iced-tea social. I heard someone yelling my name.

"Prissy, hey! It's me, Tom."

I looked up and saw two hands waving from the passenger window of a blue sports car, the driver leaning on the horn with three loud honks. I waved back with no idea who I was waving to.

It happened in a blink. The driver stopped the car in front of the sorority house where the pack of girls and I stood. He jumped out of the driver's seat and dashed across the lawn toward me.

"Hey, I'm Boone, a friend of Tom's." He pointed to the friend he'd left abandoned in the idling car.

I looked over at Tom, still clueless as to who either one of them were.

"Can I call you later?" Boone asked. He had a small notebook and a short, overused pencil in his hand. "What's your number?" he asked.

I didn't answer. Again, I looked toward the passenger sitting in his car. He was still waving and grinning. I finally recognized his face; I'd met him at summer boarding school two years earlier.

"Don't you want to know my name?" I questioned, squinting up against the hot afternoon sun.

"Prissy—I already know."

"Yeah, well, what's my last name?"

"Landrum." He was right. Again he asked for a number with a glance back toward his car.

Drivers waiting behind his blue Tornado were honking their horns over and over, but he ignored them. My girlfriends were giggling and whispering. Somewhat embarrassed by the commotion, I wasn't sure what to say. I was hesitant but gave him my phone number anyway.

Boone called before the sun set the same day. Two days later, we had our first date.

On that first date, he took me to his grandmother's winter home, Waverly Plantation, where he lived alone. His elderly grandmother (adorably called Dearsey) resided mostly in Nebraska, rarely visiting her Florida home anymore.

The stately home had a large front porch and was surrounded by five acres in a quiet neighborhood called Waverly Hills. It was far from the elements of my partying friends on the south side of town. I'd never been that far north. I wasn't even sure I'd know how to find my way back to the sorority house should I need to. If he wanted to impress a young sorority girl who lived squeezed in a one-bedroom with three other girls, he succeeded.

Born into a scholarly family, he was a direct descendent of Daniel Boone. His parents named him Jonathan Daniel Boone Kuersteiner. It wasn't long before he was just Boone.

I would learn he was one of eight children, a twenty-five-year age difference spread between his oldest and youngest siblings. His parents, lonely when their first four children left for college, had decided they'd have four more children. Boone was in the first batch.

Handsome and preppy in persona and dress, Boone had an oblong and angular face with flaxen gold hair swept across his forehead and serious hazel eyes peppered with brown specks. In silhouette, his nose looked perfect but was crooked head-on. At just over six feet tall, he towered over my five-foot-four-inch frame. The blue sports car he drove was an added attraction to his charming appeal.

I'll set the stage: a charismatic law student and an unsophisticated coed. Throw in a backdrop of comfortable elegance and give me a glass of scotch. I didn't even like scotch, but it seemed fitting, since I was out of my element anyway. We sat on opposite sofas as he talked about his family, their achievements, disappointments, and history. He wasn't boastful, telling family stories of doctors, lawyers, translators, and sail makers. I pretended I was older and chic.

An evening filled with intellectual conversation, classical music, and comfortable companionship—not to mention, scotch—was memorable and destined for success. His discipline for studying law won over my longing for college fun. The bars and clubs never once had my dime. We married two years later. I was barely twenty-two; he was almost twenty-six. Surrounded by family and friends, we stood inside the Catholic church and repeated our vows. A heavy rain, coupled with still humidity, also attended that August day.

. . . To have and to hold, from this day forward, for better, for worse, for richer, for poorer, in sickness and in health, to love, honor, and cherish, 'til death do us part . . .

I couldn't know how significant those words were.

My thoughts returned to the present as I heard Du mention bedtime. It was ten o'clock, so I said goodnight to Du and the girls. I wrapped my hands around Boone's freshly shaved face, complements of Du, and whispered words of love to him. "You make me so proud, and you're so strong and brave." It was true; he was all of it.

Du had a huge appetite and ate most anything and everything, except, of course, my health foods. Most nights he hauled his own stuff to the house, teasing me about the nastiness of my staples: tofu, rice cakes, and Ensure. He stayed up with Boone and ate throughout the night while the girls and I slept.

I never saw Du sleep. If I was up for a glass of water during the night, I would find Boone fast asleep, but never Du; he roamed around full of energy. I asked more than once, "How do you stay up all night then work all day the next day? When do you sleep? You must sleep sometimes." He would laugh and tell me he didn't need sleep.

Each night, we talked for hours and learned more and more about each another.

"Your job's sad," I told him one night. "How can you help people die, get attached, do all the things you do, and watch them die? You have a horrible job. Why do you do it?"

"I like helping people—good people—like you and Mr. Boone, Sara Britton, and Garrett. You are good people. Mr. Boone, he's a good man."

He pulled me toward him, and we hugged. I held onto this big strong man as he squeezed me tighter. I felt safe and had grown to love him, a stranger only a few weeks earlier. He knew more about my pain, fear, and loss than anyone else in the world.

His caregiving list was long: men and women young and old, doctors, lawyers, and a governor of Florida. I began to feel blessed even through our everyday sadness. Each new day, I moved through my cycle of grief while Boone moved toward the end.

It was inevitable I would become dependent on Du once I finally surrendered some of my caregiving responsibilities. He arrived early in the evenings and left early in the mornings, allowing me a night's sleep to recharge my empty battery. I longed for my previous life and envied those with casual, nonchalant attitudes, enjoying their ordinary responsibilities, pleasures, and jobs.

I remembered with longing when Boone and I were a newlywed couple standing on the threshold of our lives together, innocently gazing forward and dreaming of success, children, and a happy home. Our unblemished eyes saw clearly with no haze or halos.

We were standing on a different threshold now, gazing toward what everyone dreads. Even with glasses on, it wasn't clear what you saw or how you could avoid all those obstacles, tangible and intangible, lurking in the shadows.

I began to realize that a world ruled by cancer was inimitable. Although things remained the same in our original world—

paying mortgages, buying groceries, cooking, doing laundry and all the other things that everyone else does—we were now living with things unfamiliar. It was like visiting a foreign country and seeing the same delicious foods but now with different names that we were unable to pronounce—the same but different.

At first I didn't realize all the compartments inside a cancer diagnosis: doctor's appointments, multiple tests, bills, insurance paperwork, medications, and the endless fear clinging to you day and night, especially night. I wanted to sleep but couldn't. The nightmares intruded into my overworked mind, pushing in the scary what-ifs and pushing out any belief in the power of positive thinking or chance of success.

I knew it wasn't just cancer; it could be any debilitating illness. The disease takes on a life of its own. As if battling the sickness was not enough, life's multifaceted difficulties are married to it. Yet, for the sake of the diseased loved one, you feel compelled to pretend, so they, and you, have hope. Everyone needs hope. It may be false hope, but my flawed Pollyanna personality nudged me to believe in miracles, so I did.

One morning, as the early sun peeked through my shuttered windows and my eyes opened, the glare of dismal reality reminded me why I was sleeping alone while Boone slept in another room.

The bad thing about receiving help—physical, emotional, financial, or spiritual—is that you soon begin to count on it. It wasn't surprising that I began whining when Du left for his day job each morning. Boone was becoming less communicative and needing help with everyday basic needs: bathing, dressing, and even walking. I was okay on Tuesdays and Thursdays, since I had Betty, my housekeeper. But the other three days of the week—Mondays, Wednesdays, and Fridays—challenged me.

After a few mornings of listening to my pitiful pleas—"Please don't leave. What will I do?"—Du suggested I hire someone until he could return back in the evenings.

"You need my sister," he told me. "She's available, I think."

CHAPTER EIGHTEEN

Knives and Guns

I'D STRIPPED THE BEDS, collected the laundry, and carried it downstairs to the laundry room when I ran into Betty coming through the door. She had been working for us twice a week since the girls were toddlers. We all loved Betty; she was a breath of joy. She had been helping me with Boone during the last few months, keeping him company while I ran life's errands. I was afraid to leave him home alone the other days.

Before Boone was diagnosed, there was little conversation between him and Betty, mostly small talk when he left in the mornings. Now that Boone was home, I would often hear Betty talking to him or laughing at herself for something she'd said, and sometimes even singing. It was a one-sided conversation mostly, but no matter, she had him engaged. It was a new relationship, a genuine friendship between the two of them.

Tall and robust in stature, Betty was in a constant state of happiness. She seemed to take pleasure in the most menial tasks—washing, folding, ironing, vacuuming, and dusting—as though any and all were a personal Betty conquest.

Prior to her employment with us, she had worked for an oil family at a plantation in neighboring Thomasville, Georgia. She had perfected her skill in polishing silver and creating a delectable Southern dish called ambrosia, a dessert salad composed of fresh fruit and coconut, which she made for us each week. She lived on a small acreage north of town with her brothers and sisters. She and her siblings had their own mobile homes, all anchored in a circle on the land.

On the designated days Betty worked, she would arrive in her ancient Rambler, its dashboard dusted with stuffed animals she'd collected from McDonald's and Wendy's over the years. Betty would pull herself out of the driver's seat wearing a freshly bleached cotton uniform.

But when I nearly ran into Betty that morning, I noticed her mood was somber.

"Morning, Betty. How are you?" I asked, dropping the basket near the washing machine.

"Not so good."

"Why? That's not like you."

"How is Mr. Boone doing today?"

"Okay, about the same."

She was shaking her head and mumbling as she sorted the clothes I had dropped by the machine.

"So what's wrong?" I asked her. In all the years Betty had worked for us, I had never seen her in a bad, sad, or irritable mood.

"I been in jail." She continued sorting clothes, not even looking up.

"What?!"

"Sure was. I held a knife on Cleo."

"Who's Cleo?"

"He my husband. Common law, you call it."

I was shocked. Ten years Betty had worked for us, and this was the first time I had heard his name. She always talked about her two boys and her sisters and brothers, along with their respective families, but she had never spoken of any man in her life—much less a common-law husband. Her boys were older and no longer lived at home. I had visited numerous times and never once saw any sign of a man living there. I just assumed she was unmarried, unattached, or divorced. She never volunteered much personal information, and completely out of character for me, I never asked. I felt ridiculous to be learning something so important about Betty in such an odd way. It was surreal.

"We be off mostly. He ain't no good."

"Why in the world would you pull a knife?" *Am I really having this conversation?*

"He say he gonna kill me. Gussie called the police."

I knew Gussie—her sister—a wonderful woman I'd met on visits to Betty's house. I stood on the hard tile floor in my pink slippers and baggy gown. The laundry she was separating—whites and darks—were anything but in the right piles. I feared they were in store for a bleeding wash. I ignored my urge to snatch them and sort them myself.

"That ain't all . . . something more," Betty said.

"More than pulling a knife and going to jail?" A sarcastic laugh slipped out of me.

"Sure is. You know my boy Curtis?"

"Sure." I had heard about her boys since the day she started working for us. They were good boys.

"Mayola, his girlfriend, she robbed McDonald's last night. Um-hum. She locked them all in the cooler before she left."

"Are you kidding?" I felt like we were in an off-Broadway play reading our lines.

"She had a gun."

"What? Where'd she get a gun?"

Her bloodshot eyes and dog-down look revealed her hesitation in the words she was about to utter. "It be mine, Mrs. Prissy. It be mine." She turned from the laundry and finally looked up at me.

I couldn't speak or think, much less ask any more questions. I stood silent and waited for her to finish, afraid of what I would hear next.

"She done stole it from me."

I guess that explained why Betty used a knife on Cleo—her gun was being used for a robbery at McDonald's.

It didn't matter to me one bit. I knew Betty. She wasn't aggressive; in fact, she was just the opposite. As far as I was concerned, that scoundrel Cleo—live-in partner or whatever he was—deserved everything she gave him. I was so relieved she was released from jail. Brazen and selfish as it sounded, I dang sure needed her. No longer just a housekeeper, she had become a major caregiver to Boone those days she worked. But it still wasn't enough to get us by. Two days' help, well, it was only two days' help. I needed every day, all day, and all night. Not only that, but I also wondered if Betty was off the police radar or simply out on bail.

I immediately called Du and told him I wanted to meet his sister. After the news from Betty, I feared her two days with me each week might just be numbered.

CHAPTER NINETEEN

The Welcome Mat

SHE ARRIVED AT TEN o'clock at night, dressed in her Sunday best, as though arriving for high tea rather than just to meet with me. She wobbled in cherry-red stilettos, which matched her shiny patent purse. The woman's navy and white plus-size dress clung tightly to her large bosomed chest. The whites of her eyes stood in stark contrast to her ebony-colored skin and the crimson lipstick that creamed her lips. She wore a very large red hat, cleverly jeweled with small rhinestones, with a feather perched on the blue and white ribbon band. I would later learn this hat was only one of 147 in her collection.

She seemed nervous, believing this to be some kind of interview, unaware it was anything but. She couldn't know that, short of the deal breaker of her carrying a small axe in her red purse, she already had the job.

In contrast, I was wearing the same old flannel nightgown I'd worn the past three nights in a row, my face smeared with some expired night cream I'd found in my cosmetic drawer earlier in the day. It never occurred to me I should get properly dressed to meet someone this late in the evening.

Sallie seemed distant and unfriendly, nothing like Du. I began to think maybe she had come to interview me and realized I should get up and welcome Du's half sister with some oozing charm. I immediately jumped up to embrace her, this new life raft.

The display of affection from me, a perfect stranger, was not welcomed, nor was all my gibberish about loving her outfit. Much later I would learn I was one of the very few white women she had ever had a conversation with. Our house was only the second white house she'd ever visited.

Sallie started working the next morning, which happened to be on a Saturday. Du was working too, off from his day job. I slept late for the first time in months and awakened to the smell of bacon, so foreign to me I thought I was still asleep. I slipped out of bed, wearing my matted hair and stained nightshirt, and wandered into our kitchen. Gospel music was blaring in the background as Du and Sallie's voices filled the room in perfect harmony, both singing "Amazing Grace." As Sallie buttered Boone's homemade biscuit, I leaned against the doorjamb and listened to her last murmured verse: " . . . I once was lost but now am found, was blind, but now, I see . . . "

They had dressed Boone in starched khakis and a freshly ironed plaid shirt, along with a special hat they'd found reserved for his Texas hunting trips. Boone was sitting at the kitchen table, without a care in the world, eating his eggs, bacon, hash browns, and two buttered biscuits.

I felt rescued. Not for Boone's healing—I knew there was no hope there—but for my own personal survival. Someone was here to take care of me. I cried softly and slipped away to put on fresh clothes.

Later that afternoon, I found Sallie and Boone together in our living room. I could hear Sallie talking to Boone and eased closer to the open entry to listen to their conversation.

"Who that man?" Sallie asked. She was pointing to a framed picture of Boone on the table next to the sofa where they sat. I watched and listened, anxiously awaiting his response.

Boone stared at the picture of the man he once was. His hand patted his chest. "That's me."

"That good-lookin' man ain't you. He be clean and shaved. You be stinky."

I held my breath. Boone remained afraid of water and bathing in particular. Du and I had failed in our endeavors to coerce him into the bathtub, no matter how we tried. A quick sponge wipe was our only weapon. We'd asked Sallie if she could try to get Boone to bathe.

Sallie whispered something, and their eyes locked as he listened. I cowered behind the doorframe, a spying spectator, and blinked away angry tears. She whispered something else to him I couldn't decipher.

Boone rose from the sofa, and together they walked toward the bathroom. Sallie, the bath whisperer, had worked her magic. Bathing was never again an issue.

Sallie was a Q-tip cleaner. She spit-shined Boone and everything around him. Not only was she in charge of his care, it was clear from the start she was also in charge of my daughters and me, along with the house, laundry, and her brother Du. She gave the orders, and we listened. I was glad to obey.

We were fortunate; our house was spacious and designed in the low-country style with five bedrooms and four bathrooms. Both floors of the house had the same square footage, though it was an uncommon floor plan. The first story was partially underground, with three bedrooms, two bathrooms, a large recreation room, and a den one entered through a side door from a walkway off the driveway.

The second floor housed the main living area, incorporating the master bedroom, guest bedroom, kitchen, dining room, living room, and family room. The girls' bedrooms and the spare bedroom were downstairs. Du was appointed the spare room. He kept his personal belongings there but insisted he stay with Boone in the upstairs guest room.

"I'm paid to be with Mr. Boone. You don't pay me to sleep," he remarked more than once.

During the first two weeks, Sallie and Du would come and go just as one was leaving and the other arriving, bidding "hey" and "bye" as each passed through the kitchen door.

The rain was pouring outside one evening as Sallie was gathering her purse to leave.

"Sallie, it's too dangerous for you to be driving in the rain," I told her. "Why don't you just stay here tonight? You can stay in Du's room. He never does. It stays empty."

"I ain't got stuff, but might tomorrow."

"That's great, Sallie. It's fine with me if you just move on in." I smiled and gave her a wink.

The very next day, she did just that, arriving with a carload of stuff.

On that December day, we became a family of six: Boone, Garrett, Sara Britton, Cornelius Duhart, Sallie Madison, and me. The bells of Christmas were ringing with joyful celebrations everywhere around us except in the low-country home on Carriage Road. It was joyless, quiet, and filled with fearful anticipation of what awaited us. Only one year earlier, our home had been full of promise, prosperity, and Christmas cheer. This Christmas, we had no tree, no decorations, and no merriment. We did have help, though, and that was the greatest gift of all. I tried to be thankful. I really did.

CHAPTER TWENTY

Salvation

IT WAS THE SECOND week of December, and Du's birth mom was admitted to the hospital with complications from diabetes. Du was the oldest of all his brothers and sisters—a grown man, but still a momma's boy. There were one or two critical evenings when he chose to stay by her bedside all night. Since it wasn't her momma, Sallie took the night shift, and we could hear her snores penetrating our walls between the rooms. I tried not to think about Boone, whether he was sleeping, staring into space, or wishing for some silence.

Poor Betty, my Betty I loved, had a heart attack only a few days before Du's mother was admitted to the hospital. She thought the chest pain might be a heart attack, but rather than wake her sisters and brothers in the middle of the night, she waited for morning. By the time she called her siblings and they got her to the hospital, the damage to her heart was irreparable. It would be weeks, months, possibly never, before she would be back and able to work again. Betty was only fifty years old and was too nice to bother anyone about a heart attack, at least not until morning.

A little over a week before Christmas, the kindness cavalry delivered an eight-foot freshly cut Christmas tree to us. It had a lingering scent of evergreen that permeated our second floor. They set it up in our family room and decorated it with golden tinsel, giving it an old-world splendor. My heart was so pained during that time I can't even recall which friends delivered it or adorned it. There were no gifts under our tree, a fact pointed out to me by my friend Gayle. I hadn't really thought about it and barely noticed we had a tree. She was asking me a question as I stared into space.

"Prissy, do you have anything for the girls? They need some gifts to unwrap on Christmas morning, you know. Why not go to the mall and get them something? I'll stay here with Boone. You go on."

Gayle had offered to come over for the afternoon since Du and Sallie had taken a few hours off for their own Christmas shopping.

It really was the last thing I wanted to do, but I knew she was right. Christmas Day was only a week away, and there wasn't anything at all for the girls.

I threw myself together, chose an outfit far too large—all my clothes were two sizes too big—and took off. A year ago it would have been a joyful experience. It felt like I was going for a root canal.

I circled the lot three times before finding a space and parking my Jeep, then turned off the ignition and sat. I saw a petite woman with fire-red hair wearing her borderline tacky Christmas sweater. She walked in a quickened pace as she scanned a list she was holding. She looked frazzled. I envied her.

I closed my eyes and was lost in a memory of a previous Christmas when the kids were just little things. I tucked them in bed early—they were four and seven years old then—and scolded them not to wake us in the morning, not until the sun shone. After they were asleep, I pulled from the closets the hidden Santa gifts, along with the dozens of gifts for everyone else in our extended family. I propped the camcorder on the tripod to record the joyous celebratory morning. The girls obeyed; they didn't wake us that morning. Instead, they just opened every single gift without us—theirs and everyone else's. Name cards were scattered around our Christmas tree like confetti, along with mountains of wrapping paper.

The cold woke me up, still in the parking lot. I must have dozed off from exhaustion. I cranked the car and read the temperature inside: forty-seven degrees.

With the deepest regret, I knew then just how I'd taken our lives for granted. I headed for the scurrying shoppers and overcrowded mall, dropping a ten-dollar bill in the Salvation Army pot as a volunteer dressed in a striped Brooks Brothers suit rang the bell for donations. Boone had the same suit, and he'd rung that Salvation Army bell every Christmas holiday season for the last twenty years.

CHAPTER TWENTY-ONE

The Colonel and the Queen Anne Chair

I RETURNED HOME LESS than two hours later with only my Barnes & Noble shopping bag. Courtney, Garrett's best friend, had dropped by for a visit and was sitting in the family room with Gayle while Boone slept. Our girls were off Christmas shopping for the afternoon.

"Well, what did you get them?" Gayle asked.

I handed over my bag and watched as she pulled out my purchases.

"You got them books. That's it?" She gasped. "That's all you got?"

Was that a question or a statement? I wasn't sure.

Gayle and Courtney read the titles: *How to Cope with the Loss of a Parent*, *Saying Goodbye to the Ones You Love*, and *Grief and Its Stages*. They both rolled their eyes at the same time.

"What?" I asked.

"You must be kidding," Gayle said.

"You can't give this for Christmas. Why didn't you go to the Gap and get clothes or something?" Courtney asked.

"I just didn't think about it . . . didn't feel like it."

"I understand, Mrs. Prissy, I do. Why don't you let me go shop for you? If you give me your credit card, I'll go to the mall, get them some things, wrap them, and bring them over and put them under your tree."

"Would you, Courtney? That would be perfect." I handed her my credit card and plopped down on the sofa, exhausted.

Courtney went off and later came back with her arms full of beautifully wrapped purchases. She spread the color and gifts under our Christmas tree.

Christmas Eve approached along with my dread and despair. Du and Sallie were off to spend Christmas with their own families. Boone was still mobile but confused, tired, and edgy. As the days progressed, the subtle changes in Boone were now blatantly apparent to others. His words and sentences made no sense, and the girls and I had difficulty translating what he wanted or needed. The thought of the girls and me alone with Boone, no Sallie and Duhart to help us . . . Well, we were scared. I heard the doorbell ring.

Christmas carolers filled our front lawn. They had come from St. John's Episcopal Church and were singing "Silent Night," all of them looking like angels in white robes. I recognized the faces of fellow parishioners. The girls and I stood on the front porch, holding hands and listening. Boone lay on the couch inside, unaware the carolers were even there or that it was Christmas Eve.

An hour later, our doorbell rang again. It was our close friends Gayle and Spider Webb, along with their two sons, Sutton and Collins. The boys were the same ages as our girls; we were godparents to each other's kids. Our friendship began long before either of us even had kids, before we had even married.

"What are you doing here?" I asked, surprised to see them.

"We're here to spend Christmas Eve with y'all," Collins, the younger son said nonchalantly.

"You have your own family, Christmas Eve service at the church . . . You don't need to hang out here," I said.

All four ignored me, closed the door behind them, and walked around me. I'd never been so grateful and never appreciated their friendship more. They walked into our somber living room, decorated in a façade of Christmas cheer, and joyfully asked where the Colonel was. It was a nickname the boys gave Boone years earlier due to his strict disciplining of our two girls.

We sat around sharing stories. Boone listened but made no sense when he interjected a word or a sentence. Gayle brought gifts for all of us, though I had none with which to reciprocate.

"This one's for you, Boone." She handed it to him.

We all watched as he struggled to open it. When he finally did, he threw the gift down on the floor and began crumbling the wrapping paper, opening and crumpling, opening and crumpling, as though the noise fascinated him. We all sat in shocked silence. I walked over and took the paper from him. I am now ashamed to admit I was embarrassed.

Later, as Gayle caught me up on local news, I looked up and saw Boone standing by the Christmas tree. I thought he was admiring the gifts but then noticed he had unzipped his pants. Before I realized what happened, he had already peed all over the wrapped gifts Courtney had delivered that morning. He thought he was in the bathroom. Without a word from me, the Webb boys took charge and cleaned it all up.

As the night wore on, everyone noticed Boone was tired and disoriented. We all were. The bleak uneasiness of the entire evening was encapsulating the room, so I asked the boys to help me get Boone to bed.

As they walked over to him, each on either side of his chair, they tried to stand him up. He couldn't rise. His legs didn't straighten from their bent position. They pulled his legs straight, lifting them up and parallel to the floor, then tried to lift him up. His legs would not stay straight; they went back to their bent position. His brain, his legs, or the connection between the two was disconnected. They carried him, sitting in his Queen Anne dining room chair, from our family room to the bedroom, and rolled him into bed.

Boone never walked again.

CHAPTER TWENTY-TWO

Mad Cap

IT WAS SOMETIME AROUND the first week of January. Sallie and I were sitting at the kitchen table looking over the morning newspaper. By then she had been working for us a few weeks. She had warmed up to me. We'd become chatty, having spent so many hours together.

"Christy? I've been meaning to talk to you about Du." She was turning the newspaper page. "He ain't able to do as good a job as he could. His wife calling, aggravating him all day long."

"What?" I was in the middle of an article I was reading and wasn't listening.

"Du's wife—she call day and night."

I put the paper down and looked up. "What are you talking about? How can she aggravate him? She never *sees* him between his day job and being here all night." I had stopped answering our phone altogether. I occasionally reviewed written messages and any handwritten notes inside the spiral notebook next to the phone. Du and his wife had been married for twenty-nine years, according to Sallie. He never talked about his wife at all; I had never met her.

"You need to block her calls," Sallie told me.

"Block her calls? What are you talking about? How do I block her calls?"

She pulled herself up from the kitchen chair and brought the portable phone over to me. She was punching in numbers before my eyes even focused on the digits.

"There, I did it. She can't call no more."

I was still looking at the phone, wondering what in the world she had just punched and whom else she had blocked. I realized I had no memory of Du's wife ever calling, not even *once*.

I forgot about the phone block, never mentioning it to Du, as another week in January went by. The next time it came up was lunch on a Monday. Sallie was making Boone a sandwich. I was crushing up his next dose of wicked medication: Prednisone, the steroid used to prevent tumor swellings.

"That woman, she's still making Du crazy," Sallie told me.

"Who are you talking about?" I asked.

"They ain't got a marriage, haven't for some time. She is mean as a snake."

"Well, why does he stay married to her?" I wondered how anyone could be mean to Du. He was a saint as far as I was concerned.

"He can't pay for a divorce."

I was quiet, crushing the pills and thinking. I knew she was watching me, waiting for me to say something. Finally, I said, "Well, that's too bad, especially if he's so unhappy. I might be able to help. After all, most of our friends are lawyers, you know? Mr. Boone is a lawyer himself."

"Du would sure be happy if you could."

"I can't make any promises. I don't know. I'll see what I can do, okay? I need to talk to Du first."

Later that day, I talked to Du, and he confirmed everything Sallie had said. I called Bill Hanley, a good friend who just happened to be a good lawyer too.

Bill arrived a short time later, anxious to help any way he could. He and Boone had met in law school twenty-five years earlier. They were die-hard friends, as were his wife, Bunny, and I. We'd owned a beach house together for years. Our daughters had grown up together, even sharing the same crib, until I realized Mary Heather, their daughter, enjoyed biting chunks of flesh from Garrett's face. Bunny and Bill were devastated by Boone's illness and our current plight.

I retold Sallie's version of the story to Bill: Du had a selfish and angry wife, and he wanted a divorce. He had no funds for a divorce, so they were forced to remain married.

After I filled him in on what I knew, I went and found Du in the guest bedroom sitting next to Boone. Du was telling Boone stories as Boone stared at him, unresponsive.

My dining room served as their conference table. The lawyer and client meeting lasted just under forty-five minutes. Bill told Du he would get back to him as they shook hands. Turning his attention to me, Bill asked about Boone, gave me a hug, then left. The divorce was filed the next day.

The calm was short lived. Two days after Bill's visit with Du, Sallie received a phone call. Her son had been arrested and was in the Wakulla County Jail in a rural town fourteen miles south of Tallahassee. She wasn't told why. Sallie was hysterical and couldn't be consoled by me or Du. She left and drove to the jail to see what had happened. Two hours later she returned home.

"Lord, help him. You got to get him out, Christy."

"I don't know what he's in for. How can *I* get him out?"

Sallie was crying so hard I could hardly understand her, so I kept telling her to take a breath and tell me what she knew.

"They say he pulled a gun on somebody."

"Did he?"

"He say he didn't. He say he being falsely accused."

She and Du were both crying. Boone was staring at the whole lot of us. Did he understand what was happening? Did he want to offer advice? Boone hadn't spoken a coherent sentence in weeks, so who knew? I really was worried. The county where Sallie's son sat in jail was racially intolerant for the most part. When I'd been there in the past, I'd seen plenty of pickup trucks with Dixie flags draped on the seats and hunting guns riding passenger. It wasn't a good place for Sallie's son to spend any time.

I called the police station, but they wouldn't tell me anything. It was ten o'clock at night. There was one person I knew who might be able to help: Ken Katsaris, my friend's brother-in-law. He had been the sheriff in Tallahassee when Ted Bundy wreaked terror in our city in 1978. Ken was in charge of the case and ultimately Bundy's arrest. I called him and asked if he might make some inquiries so Sallie would stop crying. He did but later called back and said there was nothing he could do. He recommended she post bail if she wanted him released. Bail, really? I had no idea what that even meant, much less how to go about it.

All hell broke loose over the next few days. Du's mother was readmitted to the hospital. He was running between our house, the hospital, and his day job. Sallie stayed at the jail with her son, finally deeding her house as bond money and got him released. Betty's heart condition precluded her working. I was trying to handle everything else; it was virtually impossible.

I was in a daze and felt like I was living on the set of some B-list soap opera. The front-room drama was matched only by the back-room drama—taking care of Boone.

"Du, this isn't working," I told him when he finally returned after four nights of chaos and me with zero sleep. "I understand about your momma—I'm really sorry. I know you want to be with her. I understand about Sallie and that she wants to help her son. But I need help too. What am I supposed to do when you two leave with no notice? The girls and I can't do it. We can't lift Boone." I started crying.

"I been thinking about it, I have. I'll get you somebody in case we gotta be gone. Don't you be crying. I'll get him tomorrow."

The next day Du walked in our door with Willie Stokes.

CHAPTER TWENTY-THREE

A Quiet Man

WILLIE STOKES WAS A really skinny but very strong man. Du told me that Willie occasionally volunteered at their church. Willie began working for us once a week and was a gentleman of few words. There was no conversation or small talk between us on the days he worked. Since Willie didn't drive, Du was responsible for his transportation and for delegating his duties. He always directed Willie as to what to do before he left for the hospital for work or to check on his mother. Willie would sit on one of the matching love seats facing Boone, neither of them saying a word, staring at each other.

On any given day, I heard only three or four words from Willie, which were prompted by me asking a question.

"Are you hungry, Willie?"

"Isn't it pretty outside, Willie?"

"Are you tired, Willie?"

Whatever the question, he always gave a short answer.

"Yes, ma'am."

"No, ma'am."

"I sure do, thank you, Mrs. Boone."

I was unsure what my real name was anymore: "Christy" by Du and Sallie, "Mrs. Boone" by Willie, and "Mrs. Prissy" by Betty.

On one particular day, Willie finally said a full sentence.

"Mrs. Boone, we need take Mr. Boone outside. He be in this house all day long."

Wow. It was a profound statement. Something I had overlooked—we all had. Boone was an outdoorsman, had been all his life. Here he was, stuck in the house for months with peppered strangers coming and going. I decided I would do something about it, even though his wheelchair would make it challenging, especially with our living room and bedroom on the second level.

I decided I should build a deck off our family room. Then I could roll Boone out into the sunshine, where he could smell the crisp air and see the blue sky canvased behind green-leafed trees.

I pulled out the phone book and searched the yellow pages. By the first week in February, we had our deck, directly off our family room and overlooking the backyard. The man with few words, Willie, was the first one to roll Boone's wheelchair onto the deck and into the sunshine. I followed behind.

"Don't worry, honey. We didn't pay for it. My mother did." A small white lie, just in case he might still be mentally able to worry about finances or what I might be doing with our money.

It didn't take me long—a day really—to realize we had a big problem with the deck. It gave us a clear view into the neighbor's window behind us. The neighbors had no curtains, and the man of the house wore no pants, just skivvy underwear. It was not the view I was looking for. I saw him watching us from his window. We had no privacy. I called the fence company and told them I needed a quote.

The wooden fence went up two days later. I added a lattice to the top, making it even taller. I couldn't see the neighbor or his fashion anymore. It was perfect, until that neighbor knocked on my front door the next day and introduced himself.

I invited him in and offered him iced tea. In an instant, he held up a snapshot of a chair against a fence—my fence, his chair, the picture taken in his backyard. I realized too late this wasn't a courtesy visit.

"Your fence is blocking everything; it's way too high. Why'd you make it so damn tall? You need to take it down." His demeanor was almost hostile.

"I'm sorry, but our deck is on the second level. It's high, so the fence is high. We wanted the privacy."

"What privacy?" he asked, getting more aggressive.

"Our privacy." I was beginning to become defensive, something not in my nature. "I could see you, everything in your house, and you could see everything on our deck."

"You can't see in our house; we have curtains," he snapped.

I couldn't resist. My anger had been festering for weeks. This neighbor, with his accusatory complaints, put me over the edge. He wouldn't know that when he knocked on my door with his Polaroid picture, he was about to be my perfect target.

"Are you kidding me? I saw you watching television—*The Simpsons*, no less—in blue underwear. Don't tell me I can't see you. Don't you tell me you aren't staring at us. Get out of my house."

Who was I? I had never spoken to anyone that way. I never heard from him again.

Culinary angels began depositing full-course dinners they'd cooked for us, leaving them outside our kitchen door by five o'clock each afternoon. My sweet friend Rhonda set a cooler outside the kitchen door. The cooler remained there for months awaiting the gifted meals. We listened for the squeak and slam of the cooler's plastic top opening and closing. This Monday-through-Friday ritual of village nurturing continued for seventeen weeks in the winter of 1998.

It was a Saturday, and since there were other meals to be reckoned with besides dinner, I got ready to make a trip to the grocery store. Du and Sallie sat in the family room with Boone.

"I'm running to the store. You want anything?" I asked Du and Sallie.

"We sure do. There's no food in this house worth eating, Christy," Du told me, laughing. He poked Sallie on the arm.

"It no wonder you're a bag a bones, Christy," Sallie said, elbowing Du. "You need to be eating you some good food."

I was still recovering from something Sallie had told me. What little appetite I'd had dissipated after hearing one of her stories.

"Christy, did I tell you about me and Jeannette when we be sixteen?" Sallie asked me as we sat in the kitchen about a week earlier.

"No, who's Jeannette?"

"She my friend I growed up with. We always going to a food joint near her house. They sell hamburgers, best hamburgers you ever ate. Everybody go there; they stay busy because they be so good. One day we seen on the news show the place done closed up; man was arrested for feeding folks dog meat. He be stealing them from around the neighborhood. They found fur all over his kitchen."

"Stop talking, Sallie! Just stop! I don't want to hear another word." I remember grabbing Puddles off the kitchen floor and fleeing from the kitchen, Sallie's boisterous laugh behind me.

It was now five days after her tale, and I could still hardly eat anything. I tried to push the story out of my mind and continued to scribble their list on my paper: whole milk, white bread, Crisco, pigs' feet, ham hock, collard greens, and chicken thighs.

"Can you drive through Kentucky Fried Chicken, get us some pot pies too?" Du asked. I had no idea they even made pot pies. It was a high-caloric detail to learn.

Finding some of their items in the grocery store was a challenge. I had worn a warm hat covering my head and was trying to dress incognito, not wanting to see anyone who knew me. I had nothing to talk about.

As I emptied the grocery buggy and placed Du and Sallie's requested food items on the moving conveyor belt, my hands were actually shaking. I had spent most of my adult life purchasing tofu, skinless chicken breast, skim milk, lentil beans, and organic produce. It was ironic: They were healthy and eating lard. Boone was sick and eating healthy foods. It was a flawed logic I was trying to wrap my head around. Still, in my inflexible thinking, I felt as though I were buying illegal drugs and looked around to make sure I wasn't being watched. I paid the cashier and left.

CHAPTER TWENTY-FOUR

Search, Rescue, and Poof

I DRAGGED MYSELF FROM bed at eight o'clock. It was a Friday morning, and very unusual for me, I had slept in for a change. Only an hour earlier, Du had helped Boone change from pajamas into regular clothes then rushed off for his day job, leaving Boone sitting in his wheelchair. I discovered him there after I woke up.

Most mornings by eight, Sallie would have spit-shined Boone, and he would be pushed up to the kitchen table. She would be singing her favorite gospel tune and scrambling eggs or making maple-syrup oatmeal, sometimes pausing mid-verse to say a word to Boone, me, or nobody in particular. Not this morning, though. She was nowhere upstairs. I went downstairs looking for her.

"Sallie, where are you?" I hollered as I walked down the hallway toward her bedroom door. I noticed the bathroom door was shut, so I knocked softly.

"Sallie, are you okay?"

"Christy—I be sick."

I could hear her throwing up and waited for a quiet reprieve before I spoke again. "May I come in?"

"Yes, ma'am."

I opened the door and found Sallie sitting on the tub ledge, her head over the toilet bowl. She looked awful. I wiped her forehead with a damp cloth and asked her what kind of symptoms she had and when they began. Then I helped her into bed. It was clear to me she probably had a stomach virus or something she ate didn't agree with her.

I gathered a few remedies: aspirin, Gatorade, and saltine crackers. I placed them on her bedside table and gave her a small silver bell to ring if she needed me for something. I was hoping I could hear the bell, since I would be all the way upstairs.

I headed back up to make Boone's breakfast then placed a call to Du and left a message for him to call. I wanted him to know Sallie was sick and unable to work.

Two hours later, while I was still waiting for his return call, he walked in the door showing the same symptoms as Sallie. I realized neither of them would be working that day. It was going to be a long twenty-four to forty-eight hours before they could.

After preparing Boone a light lunch and getting him comfortable, I went back downstairs. Once again, I heard the sounds of vomiting coming from the bathroom. This time it sounded like Du. I went to wake Sallie.

"Sallie, Du's sick too. I need to call Willie, see if he can work. What's his phone number?"

"Ain't got phone," she murmured, still half-asleep.

"Where's he live?" I whispered, shaking her gently again.

"He can't come," she snapped back.

Du came in from the bathroom looking as bad as Sallie.

"I'm sorry you guys are sick," I said. "What did you eat, anyway? Something must have been bad."

Neither answered as Du crawled into bed next to Sallie, pulling the comforter up to his neck.

"Listen, Du, I came to ask for Willie's phone number, but Sallie says he doesn't have a phone. Can you tell me where his house is? I'm going over to see if he can work today."

"Christy, he can't work today."

"I thought he didn't work for anyone else. If you're both sick, he can work until one of you feels better, can't he?"

Neither answered me.

"Du, give me his address. I'll go over and ask him. I will ask Phoebe to stay with Boone until I get back."

Du sat up. Sallie was either asleep or pretending to be.

"He ain't got a phone and no house. He's at the shelter. He can't come here unless he knows way ahead a time." He crawled under the covers.

"What? Willie is homeless? Why wouldn't you tell me that? You've been picking him up at the homeless shelter all this time?"

"Sure have," Du replied, almost in defiance.

I shook my head and walked out the door in disbelief. Neither one of them seemed well enough to solve my current dilemma: Boone was too heavy for me to lift, and he couldn't sit in his wheelchair waiting for them to get well.

I told Phoebe I was going to pick up Willie and nothing more.

The sun was bright that February day, but the temperature was a brisk thirty-nine degrees at one o'clock in the afternoon. I turned right on Martin Luther King Street off Tennessee Street and found the Haven of Rest Rescue Mission. There were three men sitting on the stoop outside the entrance door. I parked my Jeep directly in front, climbed out, and walked up to them. I wondered why they wanted to be outside rather than warm and toasty inside. I would later learn the shelter was only open in the evenings.

"Hi there, can you help me? I'm looking for a man named Willie Stokes. Do you know him?"

"He's gone," two of the men replied at the same time.

"Do you know where?" I asked.

"Over yonder," the third said, pointing toward some empty lots. I was squinting from the glare and wind, so I pulled my sunglasses from my purse, put them on, and looked where their fingers pointed. Quite a distance away, I could see a large lot filled with people. I thanked them and drove to the lot.

There were at least fifty people, mostly men, wrapped in tattered blankets and sitting around on logs and discarded chairs. I sat and watched them all from my heated car. I wondered what Willie thought of us when he worked for us on Sundays, while Sallie and Du were at church. I thought about our comfortable sofa in front of our warm fire with soft classical music playing in the background. I was ashamed, though I had nothing to be ashamed of. Life wasn't fair. I, for one, should know that by now.

I got out of the car, gathered my courage, and walked over to the crowd where I began tapping shoulders, one by one, looking for Willie. It wasn't long before I heard his voice.

"Mrs. Boone? That you, Mrs. Boone? You got no business here," he said, startled and staggering.

I could smell the liquor coming through his pores before I smelled his breath. Willie was drunk and seemed stoned, too. His clothes were ragged and dirty, nothing like the tidy Willie who arrived on Sundays dressed so nicely. He was holding a small brown bag; it only half concealed his almost empty bottle.

"Oh, Willie, thank God I found you. Du and Sallie are sick, and Betty's still in the hospital. I need you today. Can you come over and help me?"

"No, ma'am. It ain't Sunday," he stammered.

"Yes, yes, you can. You have to," I begged, wrapping my arm around his waist and pulling him toward my car. I had not seen Willie since the previous Sunday. It was aromatically clear Willie had not bathed in those five days. I strapped him in the backseat and listened to him snore, my windows wide open, the frigid air blowing inside. I headed north toward my side of town.

As I drove from the shelter, I attempted to justify my behavior. Did I really drive to a homeless shelter and pick up a drunk, and probably stoned, man? How well did I know Willie Stokes, and was I really taking him back to my house where my daughters lived? Was he a felon? How would I know? Could he have told his friends about us, where we lived? Should I be worried for our safety? Was I just desperate or now crazy? And Boone, my poor husband, oh my God . . . What would he think? He was the most protective and cautious person I knew.

Of course, he wouldn't know. By now, he was unable to speak, walk, hear, or see.

After a twenty-minute car ride home, I was chilled to the bone from having all the windows down but was hopeful it might help Willie sober up.

I drove directly into our carport, jumped out, and ran around to the backdoor to find Willie slumped over, almost unconscious. He seemed confused and dazed, acting like he didn't know where he was or who I was. He didn't even know who he was.

I shook him. "Come on, Willie, wake up." I dragged him out, half carrying his almost dead weight through the side entrance door, not wanting anyone else to see us.

There was a bathroom inside to the right of the door. I took hím in and turned on the cold water in the shower. It was mean. He must've been freezing, but I had to sober him up and couldn't think what else to do.

"Willie, I'm leaving you in here. Take your clothes off, and get in the shower, you hear?" He looked at me with dilated, bloodshot eyes. The smell permeating the small bathroom was like nothing I had ever breathed.

I closed the bathroom door, praying he would be able to take his clothes off and step over the tub ledge to get in. I couldn't imagine having to bathe Willie. I wouldn't bathe him, or would I?

I checked on Boone upstairs and found him sleeping. I rummaged through his closet to find some clothes for Willie: underwear, pants, shirt, socks, and a belt. The only thing I knew would fit for sure was the pair of socks. Everything else would hang on him.

Willie was so skinny, and now I knew why. He had no food to eat except what the shelter folks fed him and whatever he ate at our house on Sundays. I remembered how much he always ate and suddenly felt guilty.

I headed for the kitchen and put on a pot of coffee, making it twice as strong as I normally would. I was going to sober that man up one way or another. I told Phoebe that Willie was helping Du and Sallie and would be up shortly, urging her to go on home. She left, believing all was fine.

With clean clothes and a mug of coffee in hand, I knocked on the bathroom door twenty minutes later. I didn't hear water running.

"Willie, can I come in? Are you decent?"

"Yes, ma'am."

I took a deep breath and opened the door, petrified I would see him naked. *Thank you, God.* He had a towel wrapped around his waist but was still swaying. I left the clothes on the counter, along with the cup of steaming hot coffee, and told him to get dressed and start drinking. I had an entire pot waiting for him.

Sara Britton arrived home an hour later to find Willie upstairs with her daddy and Du and Sallie asleep downstairs. She, too, was now feeling ill. I feared the stomach bug was making the rounds at our Carriage Road home. Willie was not fully sober and dressed in her daddy's clothes—two details my younger daughter hadn't noticed yet.

I still felt guilty about the cold shower I forced on Willie, and with everyone either sick or drunk in the house, I decided I would build a fire. I retrieved my down-filled vest, purple mittens, and matching hat and ventured outside to collect firewood from the pile in the backyard.

The weather was bitter cold, so I thought I would get the largest pieces of wood we had, thinking they would last longer and I wouldn't have to keep going outside for more. I used the old red wagon from the girls' childhood. I rolled the first log down, then another, watching them plop on top of the wagon. *There, four big ones—that should do*, I thought.

I pulled the wagon toward the back door, looking up toward the stairs I had yet to climb. I had a log carrier looped over my forearm, planning to haul the logs in one by one. I was already exhausted from the whole Willie adventure, but the thought of a cozy fire kept me moving.

I was a champion at building fires and had been doing them for years. I crumbled the day-old newspapers, lined them inside the bottom of the fireplace, and then laid some kindling pieces on top of the newspaper. I went back outside to get the first log and dragged it in with my log carrier. It was a huge log, lighter in color than the other three logs, I noticed. I thought it would be fine, and it fit inside the opening. I laid it on top of the kindling, lit the newspaper with my long match, blew it out, and smiled. *This will be a great fire*, I thought. *Now I just need a glass of wine.*

The fire department arrived fifteen minutes later. The billowing flames, coupled with the soot and smoke, filled our living room. I had loaded the fireplace with nothing but kindling: the huge piece I thought was a log was, in fact, kindling, and it was fused with newspaper and small pieces of more kindling.

It was a soirée of unfortunates that night: drunks and sicklings. The firemen's eyes showed bewildered amazement, wondering about the cast of characters inside the smoky house: Du and Sallie wearing their pajamas in the middle of the day; Willie swaying in Boone's oversized clothes, still clearly drunk; Boone sitting in the wheelchair with a look of sheer terror, probably from all of the above. Then there was Sara Britton and me, white lips and pasty skin in contrast to smoke and a cast of caregivers. I stood with my purple-mittened hand wrapped tightly around a glass of red wine.

I would finish it that night, along with the rest of the bottle.

CHAPTER TWENTY-FIVE

Pain, Pride, and Privilege

ON A TUESDAY MORNING in late February, I noticed Boone was a bit off. He couldn't speak, so I didn't know what was wrong. When his hospice nurse dropped by later that afternoon for her bi-weekly visit, I had her check him out. She found wheezing in his chest, a throat infection, and fluid in both ear canals. She called in a prescription for an antibiotic to our local drugstore and agreed to wait with Boone while I picked it up.

With my hair matted and no makeup, I wore a tired warm-up suit and jumped in the car to drive the six-mile distance to the drugstore. I was worried sick Boone would get pneumonia, so I drove faster than usual. As I pulled through the drive-thru window, the pharmacist said I might have to wait fifteen to thirty minutes and suggested I park and come in out of the cold. The thermostat inside my car read forty-seven degrees. I parked, went inside the overheated drugstore, and walked around while I waited for the order.

"Hey, honey, you available?" I heard a man ask.

I was standing in front of the magazines and turned around to see whom he was talking to. He was talking to *me*. This man, who looked like a rat, with beady eyes, scarred complexion, and who stunk to high heaven, was trying to pick me up. It was as though he had crawled from the garbage pile outside, slithered through the plumbing, and found himself in front of me. Was I in such disarray to be an invitation for him? I ran back to the pharmacy and felt his eyes boring through me from behind.

I paid for the medication, grabbed my bag, and fled toward my car, immediately locking the doors. Preoccupied and unnerved by the event, only five minutes en route I slammed into the back of the car in front of me. We both got out of our cars to survey the damage; it was minor. But it was a young college girl, visibly upset, crying, on the phone already calling her daddy.

"She hit me from behind, Daddy. What should I do?" she whined.

"Honey, here is my phone number. I will pay for your car, but I need to go now. My husband is very sick. I have to get home with his medicine," I said pathetically.

She relayed my plea to her dad, who told her not to let me leave. Call the police, he instructed.

"I can't wait for the police; they will take forever. Let me talk to him." I took the phone from her.

It was to no avail. He was a lawyer, and of the worst kind, from Miami. Two hours later, with a reckless driving ticket in hand, I arrived back at my house with Boone's antibiotic. Remembering the creep who tried to pick me up, I thought maybe it was time to wash my hair, change clothes, and put on some makeup. It might improve my clientele of admirers.

I learned St. John's Episcopal Church held healing ceremonies on Wednesdays. It was our church, and also where Boone had been baptized and confirmed and had served as an altar boy.

For several years, Boone taught Sunday school to preschoolers inside the small chapel. A cute, blond, four-year-old boy once asked him, "Are you God?" Boone loved sharing that story.

Since the healing services were held in this same tiny chapel, it felt like another sign to me, though I had given up on miracles by then. Even so, I mentioned it to Boone, and he seemed to comprehend and acted interested. That was enough for me to try and make it work, and a reason for him to leave our house, take a ride in the car, and see blue sky. Du volunteered to take Wednesdays off from his daytime job at the hospital and help. I needed his muscles, along with his know-how and kind manner, for this endeavor.

Our first day, I watched as Du rolled Boone's wheelchair front and center of the altar. Boone's head was bowed, his hands clasped. The priest laid his hands on Boone's newly sprouted blond hair and prayed over him as other ill ones knelt beside Boone on the needlepoint kneelers.

The chapel was beautiful, peaceful, and tranquil. I felt comforted inside the small space as I sat on one of the wooden pews, the filtered sunlight streaming through the stained glass windows. I studied all the different windows, their artistry filling each wall. The colors, design, and workmanship of each individual scene occupied my mind. One of the most beautiful windows showed Mary as she witnessed her only Son hanging in desolation. I remembered a line I heard at an Easter service once: "In sinking to the depths, he rose to the heights." I felt Mary's pain, most especially on those Wednesdays.

We stopped going when it became too hard and Boone no longer cared. The priest offered to come to our house toting his same prayer of healing. I appreciated the offer and told him so, but only on one condition.

"That would be nice; just don't wear that black shirt and white collar. I don't want Boone thinking you're here for his last rights. It'll scare him."

And he didn't. He arrived wearing his blue jeans and polo shirt looking nothing like an Episcopal priest. We would join hands in a circle while Boone sat, lay, or sometimes slept. The priest prayed out loud as the girls and I took turns wiping our tears.

On one of the last visits, his prayers were interrupted by the loudest snore I'd ever heard. We all turned around at once. Behind us we found Du fast asleep, his every snore louder than the previous. We couldn't help but laugh out loud. It seemed Du did sleep, just not when Boone was under his watchful eye.

Sallie and I had become great friends. We got to know each other pretty well, pretty fast. She told me stories. She'd previously worked in a nursing home and shared what she thought of that whole experience, saying how much more she liked working for us.

"Some people I took care of over there be white. Most of them be mean, too, Christy."

"Mean? Why?"

"Some white folk don't like black people."

"Even when you bathe, feed, and help them? I don't get that. I couldn't be mean to someone being nice."

"Well, that is you. All white people not like you."

There wasn't any defense to give her.

A few days later, we were looking at mail-order catalogs together as Sallie helped me discard months of unread, accumulated stacks of mail.

"I was skinny like you once, Christy. I was about your size just a few years ago. This weight just come on, mostly because of Duhart. He always be hungry. One time he ate my pet rabbit, sure did. Another time I caught this big fish, about ten pounds. Before I could get it stuffed, to hang up on my wall, he fried it up, ate the whole thing before I knew it."

"Really? Well, Sallie, weight pops up on some people like that." My flabbergasted reaction to the *pet* rabbit feast was concealed behind the catalog I pretended to read.

"It does. It sure did me. You think you able to help me take it off?"

"You mean your extra weight? Sure I will, if you really want to. You could do Weight Watchers; you'd love that."

I took some time to explain how it worked, having listened to more than one friend talk about it over the years. She became excited.

The next day, I picked up some pamphlets and went over all of them with her. I shopped for her then showed her how to prepare the foods and how to count points and portions. I promised to buy her a new dress when she lost fifteen pounds. That was a huge motivation. She became diligent and watched every morsel she ate. By golly, her weight started dropping right away, fifteen pounds in the first two weeks.

Just as promised, she and I headed for Lane Bryant, a plus-size women's clothing store. We were like two kids in a toy store. Sallie pulled dress after dress off the racks, and I pulled dresses from a different rack—the *sale* rack. She would pull size 24s and some that were size 26. I pulled larger sizes, thinking if they swallowed her, she would feel better. My minor in psychology kicked in, reminding me women weren't happy when a dress was too tight. I wanted to encourage her and didn't want her trying to squeeze into a dress I knew wouldn't fit.

We each had a dozen dresses in our arms by the time the saleslady showed us to the dressing room. I tried to squeeze in with Sallie.

"What you doing, Christy? There ain't room in here for both of us. I'll be out soon as I get it on."

I ignored her and squeezed in anyway. I had my Barbie doll again—her.

Sallie would strip down, put on a dress, then strut from the cramped space to the outside hall and model the dress to me, both of us laughing. I would give her the thumbs up or thumbs down. She'd come back in, strip down again, and put on another one. It was more than just fun; it was magical. The problem came when it was time to select just one dress. I found it virtually impossible to choose.

I caved. We walked out with two shopping bags full of dresses. Sallie was proud and lighter on her feet. She had found a friend, and more shocking for Sallie, it was a white woman. I felt privileged to be the one she found.

Boone's sister Karol Ann came to visit us the next week. Very preppy, she dressed the part: short plaid skirts, knee socks, loafers, and Peter Pan collared shirts. She was five feet tall, barely a hundred pounds soaking wet, and wore a size 2.

"Look at you. I sure do like that, Karol Ann, I sure do," Sallie said, referring to the cute outfit Karol Ann was wearing. "Christy's helping me lose weight. When I do, I'm gonna get one like that," she boasted.

Only three days later, Sallie walked in wearing a kilt, sweater vest, and knee socks. She was a much larger version of Karol Ann, but every bit as adorable.

As the two of us were folding laundry the next afternoon, Sallie—in her knee socks and kilt, along with her new and improved self-image and beaming confidence—asked, "Why you never be steppin' out?"

"Stepping out—what does that even mean?"

"You know, see you some men?"

Even I was speechless. "Sallie, I'm married. Boone is in the back room. What are you talking about?"

"I don't mean to make you mad, Christy. You just so pretty and nice, too young to sit around here day in and out. Well . . . it just seem wrong."

"Sallie, that's the last thing in the world I'm interested in—stepping out, or whatever you call it. I know you mean well, but honestly, that's the strangest thing you've ever said. It really is."

It was never mentioned again.

The next morning, Sallie had yet another tale for me. She was stammering, almost hysterical. She described, with great alarm, that a ghost had chased her from her room during the night. Namely, the ghost of Boone's mother, Martha Lee.

"I ain't never sleeping down there again, Christy. She come at me just because I took that needle and thread out that old chest down there."

She was referring to an antique sewing chest that sat next to her bed. In the drawers were antique sewing accessories.

"She be all over me, telling me I better put it back."

"Sallie, there are no ghosts. Trust me, if there are, they don't care if you use their needle and thread," I said, laughing.

"It ain't funny, Christy. It liked to scare me to death."

Sallie never slept downstairs again. She slept in a chair in Boone's room.

CHAPTER TWENTY-SIX

Kicking off Her Heels

THE NIGHTS WERE BRUTALLY long in the winter of 1998. Every night I cried, though no one knew. My coping skills were like steel armor, protecting me from the inevitable horror of everyday life and the unknown future. I wanted to be courageous for my girls. They were so devastated by the entire process of their father's journey toward death. I didn't want them seeing me crying, so I reserved my raw pain for the dark of night.

We had many visitors during those cold months: Boone's law partners, our friends, the girls' friends, and our minister. Their awkwardness and nervousness as they came and went was apparent. I observed them all and realized no one recognized the man they saw. He was no longer the authoritative, eloquent, and vigorous Boone they remembered, but rather a fragile, helpless, and powerless impersonator.

The worst part was my remembering, or rather, my not remembering. What was the last sentence Boone ever said to me? I had forgotten. Did I really listen to the sound of his voice, his rolled tongue, his pronunciation of every word? Did I even answer him? I couldn't remember. If I had only known those would be his last spoken words, I would have listened to every vowel, consonant, and syllable. What was he thinking now, or was he thinking? If not, what was his last coherent thought? Was it longing for a miracle? Was it his fear of death?

I noticed Boone never blinked but stared straight ahead. Could he see me, or was he blind? If he couldn't see, what was the last thing he saw? A blue sky, green grass, a red bird flying, or was it me? I hoped it was me.

He made no movement whatsoever; his arms lay motionless by his sides. There was no response when I talked to him or touched him. Was he deaf too, and if so, what was the last sound he heard?

It was all I thought about. My most torturous memory gap was my inability to remember the last time we made love. Had I known it would be our last conjugal moment, I would have cherished it. The act might have been more loving, tender, and monumental rather than just a cavalier night between a couple married for twenty-five years. The plethora of what-ifs, whys, and hows consumed my every waking moment.

I never knew for sure, but it seemed Boone was not only unable to see, hear, speak, or walk but also unable to emotionally feel anything—even me. My broken heart could hardly accept this reality. All the senses that made him alive had slipped away. He was slipping away. I began to silently say goodbye to Boone, the Boone I knew, though he was still eating, sleeping, breathing, and looked as handsome as ever.

I was afraid to leave our home even for the grocery store, though I had plenty of helpers, caregivers, relatives, and supportive friends. Boone's large family—seven brothers and sisters—were diligent visitors. It was as though they had scheduled their visits using an Excel spreadsheet, making sure the girls, Boone, and I were not forsaken.

Since I seldom left the house, there were some logistical problems, mainly my banking challenges: deposits, withdrawals, and transfers of funds. Internet banking was not the norm in 1998. Sara Britton, a junior in high school, would need unexpected cash for some school event, so I would write a check, and she'd have to go to the bank and get the cash; it was a nuisance and an untimely inconvenience.

An exceptional but humble teenager—prom queen, popular, and a frequent scorer on the girls' soccer team—she had a group of friends that surrounded her with their love, support, and attention, the very things I felt so negligent in providing at the time. She had her own car, so she was able to transport herself to and from school, activities, and other places I probably didn't want to know about.

To simplify our lives, I suggested we open a checking account just for her. After all, she would be going to college in another year. I wrote a check for $300, gave it to her, and sent her to my bank four miles down the road. I called ahead and spoke to the bank manager. She would be expecting her.

"Come right back. Don't go anywhere else, you hear?" I instructed with a peck on her cheek.

"I won't. I have to do homework," she said as she twirled the car keys in her hand and rushed out the door.

An hour and a half later, I began to wonder why she wasn't home yet. *It is taking too long*, I thought. The girls and I had pagers donated to us by a kind friend, Jack Frazee, a retired Sprint executive who wanted us connected throughout Boone's illness. I paged Sara Britton. No response. I waited ten minutes and paged her again. No answer.

I began to worry when three hours passed. I called the bank, but by then it was almost six o'clock. They were closed, and there was no answer.

Where could she be? I was beginning to panic and started calling her friends. She was not irresponsible or defiant, maybe just a little absentminded, but she'd told me she would come straight home. I knew she would have unless something had happened to her. Du and Sallie tried to calm me, but they were pacing too.

The phone rang an hour later. I scrambled to get to it, thinking it was a ransom call and someone had my daughter.

"Is this Mrs. Kuersteiner?" he asked.

"Yes, yes it is." I swallowed.

"This is Sergeant Murphy at the Tallahassee Police Department."

I didn't answer him.

"Are you there?"

"Yes, I'm here," I whispered. *He can't be a kidnapper if he's a policeman, right?* I thought.

"We have your daughter here with us. She's here for questioning. She wanted me to call and let you know she's okay. She thought you'd be worried."

"Worried? I'm frantic. Why's she there?" My voice bordered on yelling.

"Like I said, we're questioning her. A bank was robbed this afternoon; she's the key witness and giving a description to our sketch artist now."

Later, Sara Britton recounted to me what had happened. While waiting in the teller line, she started a conversation with a muscular woman standing in front of her. Sara Britton would talk to anyone, anywhere, at any time. The woman had very large hands, unruly hair, and deep frown lines burrowed into her brows. Sara Britton said the woman looked as though she had shopped at a thrift store, her blouse one or two sizes too small. The woman kept her head hung low as she waited in line, trying to avoid any conversation with Sara Britton, despite the friendly questions Sara Britton was asking her. After the woman stepped forward to the teller's window, Sara Britton waited her turn, looking down and picking a hangnail. Suddenly, the woman turned back around, a gun and a bag full of money in her hands. She faced Sara Britton, eye to eye, and almost knocked her down as she fled out of the bank with the money. Sara Britton caught herself as she heard the teller scream, "We've been robbed," and watched the robber flee.

The woman turned out to be a man, dressed in drag. She, or rather he, was captured fleeing down Thomasville Road, her high heels discarded in flight.

Poor Sara Britton never did get her checking account, at least not at that bank.

CHAPTER TWENTY-SEVEN

Bamboozled

GARRETT ABANDONED HER ROOMMATE, apartment, and carefree college life and moved back into her old room downstairs with just the basic necessities. She continued her classes at Florida State, determined to earn her business degree. She would study for hours, sitting by Boone as he slept. He'd spent two decades encouraging, instructing, and counseling her on the benefits of a college and postcollege degree. Like many girls who adored their fathers, she longed for his approval and recognition, none of which she would ever have again.

In contrast, Sara Britton avoided entering his room at all. When I would suggest she go sit with him for a minute or two, she found a reason why she couldn't. I finally realized she simply couldn't; it was too painful.

Boone worsened and was confined to his hospital bed. I argued against the bed after Du suggested it, a sterile and industrial piece of equipment sitting in a once beautiful room. The truth was I was afraid of seeing Boone lying in the stainless-steel chamber, worried he might realize it was a hospital bed and he was dying. Du won the bed battle, of course. Boone needed the bed, and I needed to accept why.

Things were up and down for Sallie and Du, too. After Sallie had posted the deed to her house as bond, her son was released from jail and the charges were dropped. But Du's mom worsened each day and was in and out of the hospital with her diabetic complications and kidney failure. One leg had gangrene and required amputation. Betty was unable to work at all, still recovering from her heart attack and the resulting damage. Willie, who continued working for us on Sundays, was brought in on other days to fill all the vacancies.

Sallie and Du seemed short-tempered with everyone, especially with each other. I didn't think much about it. Our once quiet home was now infused with an influx of people: hospice nurses, family, friends, and the girls' friends. It was a priority triage: everyone outreaching and supporting us with kindness and a ready to-do list, anything to help us survive. But it did make our life chaotic. Each one of us became subdued, lethargic, and aloof.

I was sitting on the flowered love seat reading the literature the minister had left earlier that morning. It was nothing I really wanted to read, nothing I was ready to read. My hot mocha steamed from my oversized mug, and I slurped the frothed milk that spilled over the rim. One of the grandfather clocks rang the Westminster sound, its brass pendulum chiming twice. It was two o'clock in the afternoon.

Mozart, Bach, and Chopin played softly through the surround sound speakers upstairs in the living room where I read as Boone slept down the hall in the guest bedroom. The same worn-out compact discs were played day into evening until Du and Sally finally would turn it off. I turned back to the literature and read for a bit more. Soon I looked at the clock again: 2:45. *Where is Sallie?* I wondered. She was always upstairs this time of day. I cracked the door and peeked in to check on Boone and found him sleeping. The once colorful yellow room was dark and tranquil but stale. Garrett's boom box was playing his personal favorite sound track, *The Last of the Mohicans*. I stood by the door listening and watching Boone's chest rise and fall, rise and fall. I slowly inched the door closed and went downstairs to look for Sallie, praying she wasn't sick again.

I had given Du and Sallie the spare bedroom, across from Garrett and next to Sara Britton. I suggested separate bedrooms, but they told me not to bother, especially since they worked the Jack and Jill shift and slept at different times. "One room is fine, Christy," they both said in unison.

The old mahogany bed wasn't large, but it was still a tight fit in the small room. Their closet was filled with Boone's hunting clothes and gear, affording them little space for hanging their church clothes. Sharing a bathroom with the girls, Sallie complained about the mess she constantly cleaned up: makeup, curlers, clothes, and crud. It was not a perfect arrangement for any of them, but we were well beyond anything perfect.

I could hear slamming and crying as I walked down the hall. At first I wasn't sure which room it was coming from. I knew it wasn't Sara Britton's, since she was still at school. Was it Garrett? I peeked into the spare bedroom.

"I've had it. I'm done with him. I am." Sallie was blubbering words through her crying. Her suitcase was on the bed, opened, half full of some packed clothes.

"Sallie, what in the world? Why are you crying? Wait, why are you packing?"

"I've had it, Christy. I'm done, you hear me?" Sallie's hair was wrapped in a handkerchief. Her swollen eyelids rested over her plump, round face as she looked at me. A pool of tears clung to her frowned lips.

"Oh, Sallie, I'm sorry. It's so horrible. Everything about Mr. Boone's dying is horrible. You can't leave, though. We all just have to work through this. We're at the tail end. The girls and I can't survive if you leave."

"It ain't Mr. Boone. It's Duhart. I can't take him." She threw another piece of clothing into her suitcase. I grabbed it out. "You don't know, Christy. He give me trouble all the time."

"Look, Sallie, brothers and sisters fight like everyone. You know that, don't you? I don't know what he did, but I know he's sorry." I was pleading, no longer suppressing any shame.

"Christy, that ain't it." The same piece of clothing went back in the suitcase. I snatched it back out.

"What then? Why are you mad at him? What did he do?"

"Stuff, Christy."

I was confused, trying to decide what my next question should be, trying to think how to make her stop packing her suitcase, fear settling in my stomach.

"He ain't even my brother, Christy. He my lover."

My jaw dropped, and my mind froze momentarily.

Garrett, who must have been listening from her bedroom, raced in. "Wait, wait, Sallie. What did you say? Your brother's your lover?" she squealed with saucer eyes.

Oh God. My brain was rewinding as fast as one of those old eight-millimeter movies. Sallie wasn't Du's sister, like he'd told me. She was his mistress? Wait, oh my God. All of it was sinking in—Sallie's instruction for me to block his wife's phone calls from our house, convincing me his wife was mean and hateful. Why would she do that? I had even secured the lawyer so he could divorce his poor wife; all the while, he was sleeping with his mistress in my house, and next to the girls' bedrooms.

Were they having sex down in that room? What had I done? How could I have helped do something so horrible? My brain was still rewinding each and every detail, as far back as the first time I met Sallie when she wobbled into my living room wearing those high-heel shoes.

Sallie dragged her half-empty suitcase from the bedroom and shuffled down the hall and out the door without saying another word to either one of us, not even goodbye. I could hear her sobs all the way from outside as she threw her suitcase in her car trunk.

How was it possible I had believed Willie to be a church volunteer, only to find out he was, in reality, a homeless drunk? And now, finding out that Sallie and Du, whom I believed to be brother and sister, were, in fact, lovers took the deceit to a whole new level.

Jesus, Mary, Joseph, and Du, what else didn't I know?

CHAPTER TWENTY-EIGHT

Choices

I WAS BEYOND FLABBERGASTED by the whole Sallie and Du ordeal. Garrett was on the horn calling everyone she knew to share her shocking news; Sara Britton was sharing it on the streets like any other seventeen-year-old would have. Soon word spread and my closest girlfriends were calling.

"Is it true?" Gayle asked. "What will you say to him?"

"I have no idea. I'm so shocked right now. Actually, pissed is what I am." I really was. I felt like an outsider looking into my own house. The whole sordid affair was really impossible to believe. Not the affair, per say—I knew affairs happened every second of the day—but this felt different. I was personally involved. And Du's wife just might believe I was party to their whole shenanigans.

I sat upstairs alone in the kitchen and waited for him to come home. When he did, I could tell by his demeanor that he knew I knew everything. I ejected a blast of my preaching, disappointment, and scorn before he even put his car keys down.

"How could you lie to me like that? I just don't understand."

"I'm so sorry, Christy. I really am." His was shaking his head, his eyes down.

"Du, I can't believe both of you deceived me. I feel so foolish and so guilty. Look what we did to your poor wife, a woman I never even met. I helped you divorce her. You made me an accomplice in your deceit. Don't you think I had enough to deal with, without all this? Seriously."

I walked out of the room and left him sitting at the kitchen table. My words weighed on him. I knew that much about Du. I was angry, but more, I felt hurt and betrayed.

I spent the next two hours pondering all of it, revisiting my ignorance, my inability to see the signs. There were none. I believed them to be brother and sister with different mothers but the same father. Du may have been the Angel of Death when he moved into my house, but clearly, he was no angel in life. What was I going to do? Ask him to leave? I wasn't about to cut off my own foot. Not now when I needed him most. It didn't mean I forgave either of them. It just meant I needed them—both of them.

I set up the Rule of Columns in my head. His good qualities were off the page, and this act of betrayal was just something on the wrong side of my list, the side reserved for any bad qualities. Granted, it was pretty dang bad. But still, I wanted to accept his apology and move on. I knew the good in him far outweighed this. He would have to make up with Sallie and get her back. I would tell him it was the only way he could make it up to me.

Death, or impending death, has an invisible aura. It floats around you and through you, making everything else in life seem pointless: eating, sleeping, talking, even walking. Everything is so temporary, really. Du and Sallie's charade—their lying, pretending, and deceiving—in the end, just didn't matter to me. Yes, it was awful, but as days moved on and Boone's condition deteriorated, it seemed small and inconsequential in the whole landscape. Before Boone's devastating illness, all of it might have been earth-shattering news, but in the scheme of things at this point in my life, it didn't matter anymore. I had become a different person in so many ways. My life came into perspective, and I learned what mattered; I discerned the important things from the unimportant. My judgment of others dissolved like perspiration.

On her first visit, the hospice nurse had speculated Boone had less than three weeks to live. Three months had passed since then. I contributed this miracle to Du and Sallie. They were wonderful caregivers, despite everything else they had done. In the end, their excellent caregiving of Boone was all that mattered.

My closest friends were brave enough to suggest I start making funeral arrangements: music and hymnal choices, pallbearers, eulogy speakers, a funeral parlor, and the cemetery plot.

It makes no sense why so few people make arrangements for end-of-life choices. Fact: we will die; yet, most assuredly, it is the least talked about subject—that is, until someone is confronted with it head-on in a blinding flash. I talked around it but never about it, not really. I refused to acknowledge it with anyone, not even me.

It was toward the end of February. The raw and freezing air landscaped everything a gloomy and dreary shade of gray. Du was mingling among gatherers standing in our kitchen that day. I whispered to him that I was leaving, needed fresh air, and was going to take a drive. The truth was I needed to finalize Boone's permanent resting place and set up his plot and a headstone. A committee of everyone decided this task was too personal, too selective, for any of them. I had to do it. I called Sara Britton and Garrett and asked them to meet me at the cemetery to look at markers.

We all had a job jar in those final weeks. His brothers' assignment was the funeral home arrangements. My girlfriends Gayle and Beverly appointed themselves florists and selected the church flowers and casket spray. Boone's sister Karol Ann coordinated everyone's assignments as she watched her younger brother slipping away.

Garrett and Sara Britton met me at the Old City Cemetery in downtown Tallahassee. I felt this particular cemetery location would have expressive, historical, and meaningful headstones. Since Boone was a direct descendent of Daniel Boone, I wanted his headstone to be more old world, less modern or current. I was half-crazy, as though I was decorating a room and looking for that perfect piece of furniture.

I was choosing his headstone, and he was still breathing in our home. It pains me remembering the way I felt that February day, like a cheating spouse, dirty and seedy, betraying Boone.

I walked around the quaint cemetery waiting for the girls to arrive, wondering why I had asked them to come, why I was subjecting them to such a horrid and insensitive deed. I felt like a coward, but mostly, I felt guilty for asking them to help me choose a headstone.

The Old City Cemetery in Tallahassee was established in 1829, an eleven-acre site in the heart of downtown Tallahassee. The oldest remaining marker was a simple marble slab. All the earlier wooden markers had been replaced. Buried in the cemetery were both Confederate and Union soldiers dating back to the 1860s. The markers were aged and tired, but beautiful and telling.

The girls arrived about the same time as the gentleman representing the monument company. He had driven down from South Georgia to meet us. My plan was to show him what I liked and see if he could duplicate it. Two hours and no tombstone later, we left. He suggested I take my time with my final decision, assuring me there was no hurry. I knew better.

I felt sadness for the lost souls buried there, and as I drove away, I recalled the headstones of named soldiers long forgotten. I had observed large plotted squares where entire families—mothers, fathers, children, and grandchildren—all rested. I realized each of them had endured sadness and suffering too. A different century, the same despair, the same story, with three acts: birth, life, death.

I drove toward the next cemetery on my list, the one where Boone's mother and father were buried. His father, Karl Otto Kuersteiner, had died the first year Boone and I were married. He had been dean of the School of Music at Florida State University and a concert violinist. Boone's mother, Martha Lee Boone Kuersteiner, rested next to her husband, having outlived him by twenty years.

I turned east on Piedmont Road, driving the short distance to Advent Episcopal Church and turning at Roselawn Cemetery. As I drove down the gravel road at barely five miles per hour, there was a quiet eeriness. Columns of centennial live oak trees loomed over the narrow road. I located his parents' headstones and stopped. My lungs felt strange. I became breathless, as though the air had been squeezed out of them. My heart was racing as I looked around the rolling hills at the vast array of headstones and graves. As though struck by lightning, I felt a burning sensation in my soul. I realized I'd just traveled the road to Boone's new home. I laid my head on the steering wheel and wept.

CHAPTER TWENTY-NINE

You Are Not Alone

ALTHOUGH I HAD BEEN unsuccessful in choosing a suitable headstone, I did return confident knowing I had found Boone's resting place—next to his parents. That confidence was short lived.

"I thought you knew that the cemetery was full, Prissy," said my brother-in-law Clay when I told him. "There's no room for Boone; that place has been sold out."

"*Sold out?*" I came close to screaming. "How can a cemetery be sold out? It's not a ticket to a rock concert."

"They just fill up," Clay said. "Then there's no more room, so no more plots to purchase." Clay was explaining it to me calmly. He could see I was becoming borderline hysterical.

"Where is he supposed to go?" I cried. "I thought he would be next to your parents. You're saying he has to be buried all alone?"

Clay tried to put his arm around me. I pushed it off and stomped away. I already knew I would never let that happen. I could hear Du calling me. He hated seeing me anguished and always tried to console me.

I started lobbying Boone's brothers and sisters to allow me to dig up their parents from their resting place and move them to the cemetery where Boone would be buried.

Only eleven days later, Beverly, my friend and Doncaster partner, dropped by the house like she did most mornings since Boone became ill. She delighted in describing the extraordinary scene she and her husband, Bobby, witnessed as they walked along a tree-lined neighborhood street the previous morning: two worn, unearthed caskets, both covered with hardened red clay, dirt, and years of patina, lying side by side in the back of a flat-bed truck.

The large truck drove the short distance to Oakland Cemetery, where two freshly dug graves awaited Boone's parents, along with the newly deeded fifty plots. All the Kuersteiner siblings had come together and purchased them, enough space for Boone's large, tight-knit family. There would never be a time again when a family member had to be buried alone.

Karl and Martha Lee Kuersteiner were interred to their new home that day. I knew they would be waiting for Boone. Still, it gave me little comfort.

In the afternoon, after Beverly left, the phone rang at about three o'clock. It was Alex.

"Hey, you home?" he asked. "Will you be home later?"

"Where would I go?" I replied a bit too curtly.

"I'm just checking. I have a surprise."

"What is it?"

"I can't tell you. I will say it's pretty cool."

"I'll be on the lookout. What am I looking for?"

"You'll see. Catch you later."

Alex had been wonderful on so many levels. Having grown up together, he and Boone had remained the closest of friends. Since Boone's diagnosis one year earlier, Alex seldom missed a day checking in on us, offering to help in any way possible: patching our leaking roof in the middle of the night, removing Boone's chest port, delivering and arranging flowers, ordering needed medications and dispensing them, and always counseling me. He was our champion, giving the girls and me answers to questions no others dared give.

Garrett had a date that night. It was someone new, a business student she had met months earlier named Michael Robinson. She was hesitant to leave her dad, even for a first-date dinner. I encouraged her to accept the invitation, knowing how much she needed the break. More important, she needed a distraction. Michael was to pick her up at seven thirty, so we were all waiting for him. A new face gave us something to be excited about. I had already forgotten about the phone call with Alex earlier that day.

I was in the guest bedroom sitting with Boone as he slept. If he knew I was present, he gave no indication. He remained in some other place, far away, unable to speak or even blink. He was simply there.

Garrett was downstairs getting ready for the new beau. She was trying on different outfits for her sister, Sara Britton, to critique, both of them pretending life was normal.

I could hear music coming from outside just as Du blasted into the room.

"You got to see it, Christy."

"What?"

"Come on, you got to see. Come on." Du was practically jumping up and down, his hands clasped together in front of his heart, a huge grin on his face.

I stepped outside the front door onto our porch landing. There, spread across our yard, were a dozen men, dressed in customary Scottish kilts. The sound of their bagpipes drifted across the lawn to me as I stood in gratitude. Their unique harmony and interplay of the charter and the drone left me completely spellbound. They played "Danny Boy"; its melodic sound was for Jonathan *Daniel* Boone Kuersteiner, complements of his dearest childhood friend, Alex.

Oh, Danny boy, the pipes, the pipes are calling . . .

Michael Robinson was climbing the circular stairs to our front door to pick up my Garrett for their first date. I wouldn't know he would one day be my son-in-law or that he would never get to know the most important man in my daughter's life.

I never said goodbye to Boone. He rested in a coma for the last twenty-four hours of his life while I clung to his bedside before finally climbing into his hospital bed next to him. I whispered to him, assured him over and over. "We'll be okay. We will, I promise."

We lay together into the evening, his breath labored, slow. I waited as long as I could and finally had to ask Du to help me out. I needed to pee.

"I'll be right back, sweetie," I told Boone. I kissed his parched lips, squeezed his hand, and climbed out of the bed.

I saw Du waiting for me in the hall as I came out of the bathroom, and I knew. He pulled me into his arms and held me. We both cried.

Boone had taken his last breath before the tail of my robe had swept the jamb of his bedroom door. I knew he'd waited for me to leave his bed, not wanting to share a goodbye, not wanting me to even hear it. My protector, Boone, always had his way, even to his last breath. And that was okay.

The surgeon had given him only one year to live. He'd beaten the odds, lived one week longer, but at what price?

CHAPTER THIRTY

The Toast

I SLIPPED MY DRESS off the hanger, pulled it over my head, and tried to tackle the long back zipper. I'd already run my first pair of hose and had dug around for another and managed to snag them too. The third pair survived the rough tugging, so I slipped my sheered black legs into my matching heels. I chose my favorite gold necklace Boone had given me on our twentieth wedding anniversary. I pulled my long hair into a French twist and clipped it up in a tortoise comb. No time for a much-needed hair trim.

I stared at my reflection in the mirror—the once funny and happy girl now replaced with a solemn, pale, and aged imitation. The light tap on the door told me it was time. I picked up my purse and walked out.

As I stepped out of the limousine at the church, I was shocked to see several hundred people outside, on the lawn and on the walkways, with cars still arriving. The church was already full. The small chapel was opened for extra seating with video monitors linked to the main church.

It was a smorgasbord of people from all walks of life, from both near and far away: politicians to gardeners, dignitaries to housekeepers, and even Boone's and my childhood friends. The outpouring of love and sympathy transcended anything I'd ever imagined.

My dear friends labored to create the most incredible flower arrangements on either side of the altar and throughout the 199-year-old church. The dark wooden beams, pews, and waxed floors were a rich backdrop, and the mahogany accenting the church stood in stark contrast to the hyacinths, roses, camellias, irises, and violets. Beautiful white magnolias, with their combination of green and rusty-colored leaves, lay over Boone's mahogany casket. It was so fitting for the man who loved being in the woods, enjoying nature.

Sitting directly behind us in the pew was Boone's large extended family, with Du and Sallie among them. Just as Boone's eulogy began, I heard the loud buzz of a beeper and recognized it as Du's. I knew what it meant. His mother had passed.

On that Sunday afternoon, I was told there had been only one other funeral in the history of St. John's Episcopal Church larger than Boone's. It was for Thomas LeRoy Collins, the thirty-third governor of Florida. He died the very same month, the very same day—March 12—seven years earlier. Cornelius Duhart had also been his caregiver.

Alex had the bagpipers play "Danny Boy" graveside as hundreds of friends and family stood by, the cool breeze brushing the tent as sunlight poured above us. I chose a simple headstone: a marble cross just like his parents, only smaller. After all, he was their boy. The epitaph read:

I HAVE FOUGHT THE GOOD FIGHT, I HAVE FINISHED THE RACE, AND I HAVE KEPT THE FAITH.
2 TIMOTHY 4:7

After the graveside service, everyone came to our house for the post-funeral meal, which is customary down South. The food, brought by our friends and relatives, was everywhere, spread across every counter, table, and even extra folding tables brought in that Sunday afternoon.

Du and Sallie had left immediately after Boone's service to join his own grief-stricken family. I felt lost without them as I greeted friends and Boone's colleagues, strangers known only to Boone. Over two hundred people crowded into our Carriage Road home, which was filled with flowers, music, and buffet.

Boone spent a lot of time in airplanes during his legal career. He liked to collect miniature liquor bottles, the kind flight attendants passed out in first class. He wasn't a drinker, so they just kept stockpiling, bottle after bottle, year after year. There were hundreds. We left them in a container on top of the bar in our recreation room. Boone talked about passing them out at his retirement party one day.

So on the eve of his funeral, I filled a huge bowl with all the miniature liquor bottles and centered them on a table and, next to it, placed a photograph of Boone taken the summer before he was diagnosed showing off his handsome smile. We would toast him after all, I decided.

Imagine my surprise when, one by one, everyone opened their individual bottles and realized they were drinking water, not alcohol. A nameless daughter, along with her nameless friends, had consumed the alcohol and substituted either water or tea over the last year or years. How long it took to consume it all remains a mystery, but it brought a lot of laughs to such a bleak day.

When everyone left, the house became quiet, empty, and still again. The phone rang and startled me; it was Du, sobbing. He talked about losing his beloved mother. He cried for Boone too, told me how he already missed him, me, the girls. So many months, weeks, days, hours, and minutes of tender care, guardianship, and love he'd given. Now he was brokenhearted twofold.

I asked about his mother's funeral: when, where, and all the details.

"Christy, we want to have a wake at her house, but power's been turned off for some time, since she's been in the hospital."

"Can't you call the utility company and turn it back on?" I asked.

"We could, but we ain't got that much money."

"How much is it?"

"It been turned off at least three months. About $900, thereabouts."

"I'll give you the money, Du. I'm happy to."

He came to our house within the hour, and I was so grateful to see him.

Later, I thought about his phone call and the differences—financial and cultural—between Boone, the children, and me and those who cared for us. Yes, we had a glut of drama during their employment: Betty and that wretched husband and her son's trashy girlfriend who robbed the McDonald's with Betty's gun, the discovery of Willie's homeless identity, Sallie and Du's deceitful affair, the arrest of Sallie's son. Through it all, their quality of care never wavered. It was always exceptional. My Southern caregivers, even with their flummoxing, were delightful, unselfish, compassionate people, each with their own personal problems. No different than me.

My last year had been the hardest I had ever lived, but others had it hard all the time, I realized. Misfortune, hardship, and pain were not exclusive. Maybe our social, cultural, and financial differences were not so different after all. It was all relative.

I wondered if I had given enough care, attention, and love to them or if it was just one-sided. Such thoughts kept me up on my first night all alone, a fresh widow.

CHAPTER THIRTY-ONE

Numinous Night

I LOOKED AT THE red glare beaming from my alarm clock.

How could it be two o'clock in the morning?

I rolled over and tried to go back to sleep. In the weeks since the funeral, I'd spent countless nights reflecting, wondering how it ended the way it did. In my quest to save Boone's life, I wasted it. I had dragged him several states away to a controversial doctor, delivered him to a medicine man for chanting rituals, and even paid scammers for a miracle foot soak. I stole time from him and his children. It was my denial. I felt my earlier dreams of cure were poor judgment and a huge mistake. I was consumed with guilt and regret.

Such was the way tragedy altered me. I was left a disillusioned, grief-stricken widow and mother. As I lay curled under my pink-flowered comforter, I was weighed down with self-blaming, anxiety, panic, and an overwhelming sense of hopelessness. All the emotions I had concealed so well until then had surfaced with a vengeance. My despair was visceral.

I had ordained myself Boone's investigator, negotiator, nurse, and warrior, never stopping to acknowledge my own pain, at least not in front of anyone. I would reserve my own emotional heartache for late at night, hiding in my closet under racks of clothes where no one could hear or see me cry. I needed Garrett and Sara Britton to see my strength, not a sad, weepy, and wrecked mother. They would take their cue from me. Should I fall apart, how would it affect them, their schoolwork, and their lives? My mantra: Soldier on, Prissy. Soldier on.

I had no idea who I was or where I belonged. I was no longer one of two, no longer a couple, after twenty-five years.

I was suddenly struck by this new, numbing reality. Lying in the middle of the queen-size bed, I cried, I inhaled my sob, and just as I exhaled, I was engulfed by an ineffable sense of peace. I felt a presence in my room, near me, inside me, standing over me, lying on top of me—all simultaneously. I stopped crying and sat up in my dark room. Somehow, someway, for some reason, I knew at that very moment I would be okay. I didn't know how, but I felt like I would be happy again one day. I never felt such overwhelming comfort.

Inspired by this, the next day I started planning a trip to Europe with just the girls and me. I called it a healing trip. The excitement level of Garrett and Sara Britton, on a scale of one to ten, was zero. Nonetheless, I threw myself into the arrangements. It was a Band-Aid for my broken heart, and the tasks involved were easier than the alternative: counseling, nurturing, and time.

I decided to redeem all of Boone's frequent-flier miles he'd accrued over his legal career. He and I had planned to use them for our twenty-fifth wedding anniversary trip. Even though all the booze was gone from his miniature bottle collection, we still had all the miles, enough for a full month of free travel for his daughters and me including airfare, hotels, transfers, and tours. We departed four months after Boone's funeral.

We arrived in Amsterdam on a July morning, the temperature, a brisk fifty-eight degrees, contrasting with the ninety-eight-degree stifling heat at home. It was still too early to check into our hotel, so we left our bags with the desk clerk and ventured out for a short boat ride. I wanted the girls to get acclimated to the city.

The boat had moved over the smooth waters less than two hundred feet when I noticed Sara Britton crying. It was a quiet sniffle as she tried to cover her eyes. I watched discreetly, not wanting to make a scene or embarrass her. The girls and I stepped onto the dock an hour later. Sara Britton had changed entirely. She was lethargic, withdrawn, and pale.

"What's the matter?" I asked.

She didn't answer.

"Sara Britton, sweetie, are you seasick?" I knew it wasn't likely; there had been very little motion in the boat.

Still, she didn't answer. She stared ahead.

Garrett and I turned around to see what she was focusing on, but there was nothing obvious.

After the boat returned to the dock, I hurried her to our now available room where she climbed right into bed and fell asleep. I was pretty sure the jet lag had taken over and she would be fine after a nap. Three hours later, I woke her. Garrett and I were already dressed, ready to go for the prepaid tour awaiting us.

"I don't want to go. Leave me alone," she screamed.

"Why don't you want to go? Are you sick?"

"Just leave me alone, p-l-e-a-s-e!"

We looked on, shocked.

"What is it, honey? It will be fun. Getting out in the sunshine will wake you up, help with the jet lag," I said.

She sobbed, wailed. Her whole face twisted as she cried. Garrett and I took turns trying to console her. I called and canceled the tour. Another two hours passed before I approached her again, suggesting we get some food. She remained quiet and withdrawn. I lost patience.

"I've paid good money for this trip. We're getting out of this room now," I snapped.

"I can't . . . I just can't." And then, "When I sat next to that man on the boat, he had Daddy's hands, just like his. I felt like I was sitting next to Daddy. I miss him. I miss him so much." She wept in heaves.

Three days later, she was still in bed. I missed Du and Sallie and realized they would have known what to do. I felt helpless. We should have been in Florence, Italy, according to my itinerary.

I spent hours changing flights, hotels, and tours, finally realizing she needed a doctor. She was practically in a catatonic depression, refusing food or even to leave her bed. Seeing the man's hands had created some delayed grief reaction. I wasn't competent to deal with whatever it was. I had no idea what to do or who to call. I ran downstairs to the concierge.

"I need a doctor, please," I demanded, trying to hold myself together, not wanting to act like some hysterical American. "Can you help me?" I pleaded to the concierge.

"What tis de pro-b-lem?" he asked in heavily accented English.

I told him a condensed version of the previous days' happenings. Okay—I told him much more—all the way back to Boone's diagnosis. He was on the phone calling a physician when I heard a man's voice behind me.

"Prissy, is that you?"

I turned around. Standing next to me in the lobby were Ben and Susan Bailey. Ben was one of Boone's former fraternity brothers. We both had FSU football season tickets, and Boone and I had spent years sitting next to them at games. They were on vacation—in our hotel—at that very moment. It was as though Boone had willed it. I cried as they reached out to me.

"Maybe I can help, Prissy," Ben suggested. "Do you mind if I talk to her?"

I took him up to our room and, as much as I wanted to listen, left him alone with my daughter. Later, when I checked on her, she said she was feeling hungry. I didn't know what Ben had said. Maybe more than anything she just needed to talk to a man who was close to her father. I will always be amazed we found him, and I will never be able to fully express my gratitude to him for being there for us and for saying the right things to Sara Britton when she needed it the most.

We checked out the following day to catch up on lost time. Our first stop was Hotel Caron de Beaumarchais in Paris. It should have been a traveler's heaven, but even with Sara Britton's recovery, we were still all just putting on happy faces over our sadness. We toured every tourist attraction, including Versailles, and ate at umpteen bistros and cafes. We visited every attraction I could schedule as I tried to keep us going and cheered. But there was no excitement, no joy. It was no fun, period.

We stayed three nights then took the bullet train to London: theater, British charm, and red double-decker touring should do it—plus, they spoke our language! No luck. There was still grief and sporadic tears from the girls.

From London, we took a train to Arles, Avignon, and Aix-en-Provence, France, which was a more relaxed segment of the journey. I felt sure this would be the turning point. We would marvel at the culture, scenic surroundings, and delicious foods. Not so. A week after lingering on hammocks and strolls with local villagers, we left. We were headed for the country of love: Italy.

When we arrived in Florence, I realized for the first time since leaving the United States that we were all happy at the same time. This was it; finally, we'd turned a corner. We ate pasta, gelato, and strolled through the markets with hunger and joy. We checked into Hotel Mario, Room 16. I remember only because I spilled an entire bottle of Chianti on the Oriental rug before I even unpacked. I did offer to pay for it at checkout.

We continued to have fun and laughed. Maybe our trip was healing us after all. After two nights in Florence, we took a train to Venice and checked in to Hotel Flora near St. Mark's Square. I loved Venice. I had been three times before and couldn't wait to show them.

"Come on. I want to show you where daddy and I stayed when we came," I said as we headed to Hotel Danieli, with its opulent décor and sweeping views overlooking the Venice lagoon. The hotel was in the heart of the city, near St. Mark's Square, the Palazzo Ducale, and the Bridge of Sighs. Boone and I had spent a week in the breathtaking hotel, and I thought the girls would love revisiting it with me. It was a big mistake.

Their moods shifted again at the reminder of their father. I felt like we were in a game of monopoly: two moves forward, one move back. Venice was a wash from the moment we stepped into the lobby of Hotel Danieli.

It was our twentieth day of travel, and we were packing for checkout of Hotel Flora. I was so looking forward to our next segment—Vienna and Salzburg. I loved Austria and so had saved the best part of our journey for last, booking the finest hotel our miles could redeem. We would travel from Vienna on to Germany. I was so excited, blabbering about all the scheduled sightseeing tours, museums, and the glamour of Viennese life. I looked over at my daughters sitting on their beds and gazing out the window, uninterested in anything I was saying. It was a defining moment. I picked up the phone and booked our flight home.

CHAPTER THIRTY-TWO

Sink or Swim

IF LOSING BOONE IN the spring was devastating, the summer reinforced my despair. When we arrived back to the States from our failed European healing trip, that old saying "Bad things happen in threes" proved true. In our absence, a pipe burst under our house, rupturing our foundation. Hundreds of gallons of water flooded the entire first floor. We had to move out.

It wasn't enough, nope. In addition, the stock market took a nosedive. I lost 40 percent of Boone's life insurance. A few days later, I discovered thousands of dollars had been stolen from my checking account. All three events occurred at record speed. It was a low point.

When the renovating nightmare was over, Sara Britton and I moved back into the house. I had been staying with my mother, and Sara Britton had stayed with a friend's family. Garrett was now living in a small, affordable house I'd purchased for her.

It was a Monday morning in early January, and I ran to answer the ringing phone, my third call of the day. It was from Garrett; the earlier two had been from Sara Britton. She had a bad habit of calling me from the downstairs phone line to the upstairs line; it was easier than walking upstairs.

"Hey, Mom, what's up? What are you doing today?" Garrett asked.

Each daughter taking turns—the same questions, different dialogue—all day. I was grateful but knew they needed to enjoy their own lives: school, friends, and boyfriends. They deserved a piece of normal but remained worried about their mother.

After hanging up with Garrett, I sat on the couch and stared at the muted TV. I wouldn't have it any longer. My daughters needed to picture me in a different way, a new way, and not as just their widowed mother who was home alone most of the time. Scooping Puddles off my lap, I turned off *Wheel of Fortune* before she won the car. I needed hot tea while I pondered my life, or what was left of it. By the time my water boiled, my mind was made up. I picked up the phone and made the call I'd been thinking about since Boone died.

The sun was bright, the sky silver blue with white swirled in an abstract design. I stood on the steps of the Florida State Capitol, the same steps Boone stood on every year. It was the opening day of the legislative session, and it was all foreign to me: government, politics, bills, legislation, and law. I watched everyone running around me in expensive suits, carrying Italian briefcases and an entourage of interns trailing behind them. I felt like an idiot, mustering my courage to climb the capitol stairs toward the doors of the massive white building.

"I'm so mad. Damn you, Boone. You should be here and not me. I hate this stuff." I continued my angry whispers as I ascended the stairs.

Steps away from the executive office, I was wearing my new cream suit and three-inch heels. Two weeks earlier, on January 5, 1999, the forty-third governor of Florida, Jeb Bush, had been inaugurated. I was wondering if he felt nervous his first day in his new suit. Surely, it was new. *Remember what you've accomplished, Prissy. This isn't any harder.*

I walked through the historic hallway then down a long corridor. The waxed marble floors echoed a clicking sound from my new stilettos. I felt small, lost under the elaborate domed rotunda, the images of the Sunshine State covering a large wall. I admired the beautiful murals by Florida artist James Rosenquist but felt invisible among the thousands of scurrying suits, each one with their own agenda.

I left the plaza level housing the governor's actual office and took the elevator to the second floor where the legislative and executive offices were located. I found the numbered door matching the scribbled note in my sweaty hand. I held the handle a few seconds longer and reminded myself again, *You are qualified. You are qualified.* I took a deep inhale and walked in.

Jim Smith, former attorney general of Florida and former Florida secretary of state, recommended me for the position. It was nothing fancy. I didn't care. I would be working for the deputy general counsel to Governor Jeb Bush. Executive administrator was the title and sounded important but was far from it. I was just a secretary with a fancy name.

The butterflies were side-sweeping each other in my stomach. My painted fingernails looked too colorful as I extended my clammy hand to the pretty girl sitting at the front desk. I introduced myself with a parched throat, my voice sounding foreign to me. I flashed a smile after I gave my name to her. There was no reciprocal smile from the pretty one, only two unfriendly words, "Follow me."

My racing mind reminded me again, *You have a master's degree from Florida State University, worked until the day Garrett was born, chaired committees, worked in the Junior League, ran a household for twenty-five years, Prissy. You are qualified.* I didn't believe it, though.

Frank Jimenez, deputy general counsel, stood up to greet me. He extended his hand with an engaging smile. He was in his late thirties, handsome, articulate, and energetic. I knew I liked him right away. We began our conversation with small talk and niceties, moving into the interviewing segment. I assured him I had computer skills and was proficient in typing, phone call etiquette, and legal terminology.

Frank made my interview almost comfortable. I learned that day that he and Boone had the exact birthday. The odds were one out of 365. I believed it was a sign and no coincidence I should be exactly where I was. I started work the next day, and after week one, I was in the groove of my new routine.

"Prissy, I need to you send this letter to Judge Somebody and blind copy it to Judge Nobody, okay?" Frank instructed, handing a document to me.

I stared at him from my squeaky sprung chair, pulling the silk skirt over my exposed knees.

"It's urgent."

Everything was urgent in that office.

"Sure." I began moving papers around on my desk, stacking his letter on top. I could feel him watching me, perhaps waiting for my response.

"Why do you have that face? You know what a blind copy is, right?"

I stared back, formulating an answer in a snail's fashion. Too late, I suspected.

He sighed.

Did he really just sigh?

"Prissy, come in my office and shut the door."

I was already orchestrating my response when he turned around, motioning me to sit in the chair in front of his desk.

"I thought you told me you had worked as a legal secretary."

I shifted around in the hard chair. I never liked any of the office chairs. The state needed a new decorator.

"Well, I did—sort of. You see, I was married to a lawyer for twenty-five years. He told me what to do every day. I think that qualified."

He shook his head left to right and back again then hung it down and stared at papers on his less-than-immaculate desk. I waited, still thinking of some defense for my small white lie. Okay, a big white lie.

For some reason, he didn't fire me. He even laughed. We were a good fit from the beginning. Anything I didn't know I soon learned.

Florida has the third-largest capitol building in the United States, a twenty-five-story building, if you include the three floors underground. My cardio workout each day was climbing the twenty-two flights of stairs from our second floor to the observation deck on the twenty-second floor. It is 512 feet above sea level, and on a clear day, you could see all the way to the coastline. On a few occasions, Governor Bush climbed with me, his entourage following behind while briefing him. I liked Jeb Bush then and still do. He is friendly, interesting, extremely smart, and funny. He didn't seem full of himself or pious from his political success or social privilege.

I learned invaluable lessons working in the governor's office. In my earlier role as a stay-at-home mom, I wasn't privy to the dance steps on the political ballroom floor, the creation of bills, passing of laws, and governing of the state. I was as far away removed from politics as an atheist is from church. I witnessed the good in many but also the bad in some. It was an eye-opener for me, a virgin to the political arena. I believed if I was nice to everyone, they would like me. That wasn't true.

In those first weeks, I wouldn't know why others in the office resented me. I would later learn I was notched above others, after all their years of commitment and loyalty. I was a naïve homemaker who was fortunate enough to have an important friend. I was qualified and competent in many ways, and I did an excellent job for Frank and the governor. But, so might someone else.

"I love your blouse. Where'd you get it?" I said to one of the girls.

"How was your weekend? Did y'all go to the beach?" I asked another.

I got one-line answers with few smiles. Well, really, no smiles.

"Would you mind showing me how to insert this on the Excel spreadsheet?" I asked a third. She showed me with a sour face. I hesitated asking again, even though I was completely lost. I stayed up an entire night and learned the Excel computer program. I could spread anything the next day. By the end of that week, I was in charge of documenting each passed and vetoed Florida bill during the legislative session.

On a Tuesday morning around my fifth week, I laid my purse on my desk in my cubicle and went to check on Frank. He wasn't in yet. I turned around to find Sandra standing at my desk. She handed me a package of Ferrero chocolate candy. Was she smiling at me?

"What's this?" I asked.

"Look, I tried not to like you, I really did. You came in here from nowhere, took this job. It wasn't right. I can't help it, though—I like you. Here you go, a peace offering for the way I've acted."

It was a wonderful morning, the first in a very long time.

CHAPTER THIRTY-THREE

The Meaning of Time

THE SUN WAS BRIGHT, the glare bouncing from the dashboard of my Jeep. I looked at the thermometer gauge above my rear-view mirror: ninety-one degrees in April. Ugh. With the drenching humidity, it felt twenty degrees hotter. How could we have jumped from cold to stifling heat in just three days?

My white organza dress clung to my fake-tan legs, perspiration collected under my arms, and more dripped between my breasts. I reached down and switched the air conditioner to pull cool air through the lower vents. I needed the sucker blowing up my skirt, not just in my face.

The wedding started at three thirty, and it was already after two. I was anxious to get to the church, since I was the maid of honor. We didn't have a rehearsal the night before, so I wondered how it would come together. I had never been in a wedding without a rehearsal, but I had never been in a wedding like this one either.

"Right here, Mom," Garrett directed from the passenger seat. "Take US 90. This is exit 209B. Get off here."

We were traveling on I-10, both my girls giving me directions at the same time.

"Stay on this road."

"Turn here, then left."

They argued about which exit to take then finally agreed on one.

We were looking for Union Branch Missionary Baptist Church, on the east side of Tallahassee. We finally saw Wadesboro Road and turned right. Bone-dry brush from weeks of no rain scraped our car as we drove down the long dirt road. Ahead, I saw a small white church but no one was there. Not a single car.

"Oh my God, we're at the wrong place," I said.

"Mom, this is the right place. Look, here's the invitation. This is it. This is the church," Sara Britton told me.

"Where are the people? Why is no one here? Wait. Is this the right day? What's today?"

"Mom, this is the right day. Calm down. They will be here in a minute," Garrett replied calmly.

"The wedding starts in an hour. How can it be vacant?" I looked down at the invitation for the umpteenth time.

CORNELIUS DUHART AND SALLIE MADISON
REQUEST YOUR PRESENCE
CELEBRATING THEIR MARRIAGE
ON
APRIL 11, 1999
3:30 P.M.
UNION BRANCH MISSIONARY BAPTIST CHURCH
9701 WADESBORO ROAD
TALLAHASSEE, FLORIDA
RECEPTION TO FOLLOW
SOCIAL HALL
MICCOSUKEE, FLORIDA

Du and Sallie were getting married. Sallie asked *me* to be her maid of honor, insisting I wear a white dress to match hers. I had borrowed the vintage dress I was wearing from my mother's closet.

"Christy, when we get married, we want it at your house. What you think about it?" Du asked more than once.

"Sure you can," I told him.

They spent the next year planning their big event: perfect date, wedding dress, bridesmaids and their dresses, groomsmen and their tuxedos, rings, invitations, flowers, and wedding music. Most everything was put on layaway, paid off slowly, dollar by dollar. Any balance left was put on their credit cards.

As promised, I offered to host the wedding at my house. But by then, the idea seemed less important to either of them. They decided on a traditional church wedding. So here we were, finally, on their wedding day. I felt privileged to be included and invited my entourage of supporters: daughters, mother, sisters, and friends Gayle, Spider, and Phoebe. They arrived about the same time we did. We mingled together around our cars, waiting and watching for some sign of life.

Suddenly we heard a vehicle. A large sedan with a rattling and hissing sound was approaching us. The car eased up the road and passed us. I saw a buildup of black soot on the muffler and the contaminants blowing out. The woman behind the wheel looked dwarfed, her head barely above the steering wheel.

She was wearing a large hat with netting. She pulled in, backed up, pulled in again, backed up, and then stopped. She got the aged Lincoln just where she wanted it—in the middle of the road—and got out.

I scurried over. "Are you a guest for the wedding today?" I asked.

"No'm. I'm Sister Mayetta, here to get the church ready."

"It's three o'clock. Doesn't it start in thirty minutes?"

"Yes'm. It sure do."

The girls and I stood behind while she unlocked the door to the small church. When she pulled it open, accumulated heat rushed through the opened door, blasting us from inside.

We stepped in and watched as she rummaged through a closet, her purse still dangling from her arm. First, she stuffed plastic flowers into bins nailed to the end of each pew. Then she dragged a large roll of red plastic from the closet floor to the center aisle, unrolling it toward the front with the toe of her right shoe. She grabbed more flowers from the closet, arranging them in a vase on the front altar. Hymnals were removed from the closet shelf and distributed along the seats of the old wooden pews. A cardboard fan with a wooden stick attached was laid atop each hymnal. She had the entire place decorated in no time.

Sister Mayetta limped toward the old organ in front of the church. She placed a selected sheet of music on the holder. The scraped and worn wood floors, coupled with the patina from the aged pews, complemented the charmed setting of the small church. There was no air-conditioning.

Then we heard cars coming, loud music blaring, horns honking, and shouts and screams through the open windows. We walked outside to find the wedding party. The groomsmen wore white tuxedos with lavender vests and cummerbunds. The bridesmaids wore matching formal lavender dresses.

I walked back inside the church. The artificial flowers placed on the pews and altar, coupled with the red plastic running down the center aisle, gave the hot room a spring theme. I thought the lavender and white would tie it all together—a coordinated bow on the carefully wrapped package.

The only people sitting in the pews were my mother, daughters, sisters, and friends. They were dripping wet, fanning themselves with the complementary cardboard fans. It was four o'clock, thirty minutes after the appointed time on the inscribed invitation, and still no sign of the bride and groom.

I followed the wedding party to a small building around back and went inside. Box fans were blowing. Everyone was mingling, chatting, and laughing among themselves—everyone but me, that is. I found an empty chair and sat, pretending to be searching for something in my purse. I knew no one and saw the women whispering and looking over in my direction. I mustered some courage and moved closer to introduce myself.

"Hi, I'm Prissy," I said, extending my hand.

"Umm hmm, we know who you is. Sallie told us all about you," a heavier lady replied. She didn't smile and didn't volunteer her name.

"It's nice to see you all. Sallie always talks about you guys, too," I said. She *hadn't,* but I was desperate for something to say. Their chill in that sweaty room was making me nauseous.

"I thought the wedding started at three thirty. Where is everyone?" I asked no one in particular, hoping someone would answer. No one did.

I was still trying to figure out how it could be 4:15 with not one sign of the bride or groom. I went back to my spot away from the women, since no one was acknowledging my presence anyway. I had my eye on the door, waiting for Du or Sallie to rescue me.

"Don't be worrying yourself about them women not talking to you," one of the groomsmen told me as he tilted his head in the bridesmaids' direction. He was a tall man with a kind smile. "They're just mad at Sallie because you her friend now; you her best woman." He extended his hand toward me. "My name is Clyde. You is welcome here."

I smiled and grasped his strong hand just as Du walked in.

"Hey, Christy." With a grin wider than his cheeks, he grabbed me in a bear hug. I saw the lavender women's glare.

"Du, where have you been? Where's Sallie? Why hasn't the wedding started? I've been here since two thirty. It's almost four thirty." I was scolding him, looking at my watch, not realizing how frantic I sounded to everyone.

"Christy, just because it say three thirty don't mean three thirty. Everybody know it mean get here close as they can," Du said.

"What? That makes no sense to me. Why would your invitation say three thirty if you mean five o'clock?"

Du had already walked away and was shaking everyone's hands before I finished my question. It was then I saw Sallie coming through the door, drenched in sweat. She was wearing her wedding dress with a full train. The lavender "ice cubes" jumped up and surrounded her. I waited on the far side of the room, wanting her to find me, hesitant to approach. When she broke away from her friends, she came over and we hugged.

I wiped her sweaty brow with a handkerchief I'd pulled from inside my purse. "Where have you been? You're so late."

"I've been setting up for the party all day. I done took food, plates, cloths, drinks, just about everything."

"I would have helped you. Why didn't you call me? You're the bride. Brides don't set up for their own party." I felt terrible for her. I felt terrible for me, too, and was close to telling her my own circumstances with the lavender girls when I heard Du clapping his hands.

"Come on, everybody. Sallie's here, so you need to go on over to the church."

Sister Mayetta was waiting for us and ushered the wedding party inside the sweltering one-room church. Two rows of lavender dresses, vests, and cummerbunds were lined up in front of the congregation. I stood centered in the middle of the large wedding party. I looked for *any* familiar face in the packed church and found them in the last two rows. My family and friends were all smiling at me with wet hair, red cheeks, and drenched clothes. They had been waiting over two hours.

The hand bell rang as a young voice chanted, "Here come the bride. Here come the bride."

A boy, about five years old, his smile captivating the audience, was standing at the back door ringing the bell. His miniature tuxedo, matching the groomsmen, swallowed his small frame as his tiny shoes brushed over the red plastic. Everyone stood, and the young boy, with the biggest grin in the room, moved aside for the bride to enter.

Sallie was beautiful in the plus-size wedding dress she'd spent a year paying off. The organ played Wagner's "Bridal Chorus" from *Lohengrin* as she walked to Du, her long train trailing behind her on the surrogate red carpet. I couldn't stop crying.

After the service, we attended the reception at the social hall in Miccosukee, a short drive away in another small community.

My entourage of supporters were exhausted from the long-awaited wedding, which, by the time it was complete, had added up to four hours, but they followed the girls and me to the final celebratory event.

The wedding party was grouped at one large table centered in front of the reception hall. I sat in the middle of them. Garrett and Sara Britton sat at another table with my friends and other family members. I was relieved to see everyone acted welcoming and kind to all of them. The other end of the room was filled with every conceivable type of food one could imagine: bowls piled high with rice, macaroni and cheese, acre peas, green beans, and black-eyed peas; platters of chicken, beef, and pork; and baskets of biscuits and rolls. Another table was filled with cakes, pies, cookies, and soda pop. It was a dry reception. I could have used a real drink by then.

"I need everybody's attention," Du announced, tapping his knife against a glass. "This dance is dedicated to two people we sure do love—Mr. Boone and Christy."

The sound system started playing "Minuet in G" by Johann Sebastian Bach. It was the song I played every day during Boone's last few months alive.

Du and Sallie moved to the center of the empty dance floor and began their waltz. Their grace, poise, and perfection awed me. They had been practicing the dedication waltz for over a year.

CHAPTER THIRTY-FOUR

Stepping Out

JUST HOME FROM WORK, I kicked off the four-inch heels I was still trying to break in, knowing I never would. I poured a glass of wine, another new "me" habit, and answered the ringing phone. It was Carole; she was a close friend and the wife of the former attorney general who had so graciously suggested me for my current job.

"Prissy, I've got someone I think you should go out with," she told me.

"I'm not sure about that—not sure I'm ready to date, Carole."

"You need to start going out. It's been over a year, Prissy. How about just dinner? He's nice, I promise."

"I'll think about it, okay?"

The politics of widowhood are as predictable as the politics of government. A man's wife dies and he becomes a widower, embraced by a mournful village and included in cocktail, dinner, and Christmas parties. The casserole ladies will swarm his door after the first week. But men don't make casseroles, so widows stay hungry.

Many widows say exclusion begins the day their husband dies. It happened to my mother after my father died. Only after the cocktail or dinner party had occurred would she learn she had not been invited. I remember Boone telling me it was because she was beautiful. And she was that, for sure. Yet I didn't buy his theory.

"Wives don't want her around without your dad," he said.

I encouraged him to tell her his theory, believing it might soothe her hurt feelings. I had a different take. Mine involved dining room chairs and awkward numbers. If the hosts added another couple and included my mother, it involved dragging an extra, mismatched chair from another room to the dining table, ruining the hostess's overall look and arrangement.

We each told my mother our theories, not sure which, if either, was accurate.

After living in the same small town for forty years, my mother moved from Lake City to Tallahassee one year after my father's death. Her identity lost in the sixth decade of her life, she was no longer the big fish in a pond, just a goldfish in the ocean.

I wasn't the typical widow. My friends hadn't left me behind or excluded me. On the contrary, they made sure I was never left out, inviting me to parties, lunches, and calling me on the phone. I appreciated it, yet it was the same friends, the same life, but without Boone. The void and vacancy engulfed me as everyone moved on. I knew they missed him too, but they'd remained the same and I was different. I felt misplaced. Odd gal, excess baggage, fifth wheel—every adjective and description heard over the past years from others widowed was now me. My newly crowned title—widow—called for courage. In preparation for college, Sara Britton had moved in with Garrett. I realized I was forty-eight years old, living in a 4,800-square-foot house, and alone. I had never lived alone, going from my parents' house directly to college dormitories, a sorority house, marriage, and life with Boone. No space in between. It was a new feeling, a liberated one.

I'd seldom spent any real time with myself and began to enjoy my own company. I looked forward to my nights of solitude, sipping a pinot noir, listening to Mozart, Bach, and Peter Cetera as loud as I wanted, as late as I wanted. Sometimes I'd grab my purse at eight in the evening and head to my favorite bookstore to browse, with no one to tell, ask, or justify my whereabouts to. It was a novelty, and a good one.

I gave in to Carole and decided to go on a date with Joe. Carole had said he held a powerful position in the legislature. It meant nothing to me. I was illiterate in political positions and rankings. I stepped into my pink and green sundress. My legs were tanned and muscular from weeks of capitol stair climbing, along with my new favorite exercise, Tae Bo. Looking in the mirror, I felt like an awkward and self-conscious schoolgirl waiting for her prom date. I hadn't had a date in almost twenty-nine years. I splashed on my favorite perfume as the doorbell rang.

He was nice-looking, in his early fifties, with brown eyes and a smile baring bleached white teeth. I noticed immediately he was wearing a sweater vest, something Boone never owned. I was comparing. He wasn't very tall, under six feet. Boone was much taller. Still comparing. I invited him in, feeling like someone else behind my own skin. I had to remind myself to follow my instincts and give him a chance. *Remember your Rule of Columns, Prissy.*

Joe glanced at Boone's portrait-sized photograph sitting on the easel, centered atop the baby grand piano. He sat next to me, both of us now facing the picture. Ridiculous as it was, I felt like an overdressed adulterer as Boone watched from his position on the piano.

I started making my list of flaws: the vest, his height, his shoes, his hands. He wasn't Boone. I wanted him to leave but knew no graceful way out of the corner I was in.

After twenty minutes of superficial small talk, him seeming too comfortable on the couch next to me, he finally suggested, "We should go if you're ready. I've got reservations waiting."

Please don't let it be where Boone and I went. I was too afraid to ask and just wanted to go and get back home. Damn my Rule of Columns.

Despite my misgivings, I began to relax once out of the house. Joe was a good conversationalist, engaging, funny, and complimentary. In the restaurant, I noticed everyone coming up, shaking his hand, slapping him on the back. They talked law, politics, upcoming meetings, bills and laws, and future lunch dates, then he'd return to me and our conversation. I talked Boone: cancer, treatment, caregiving, death, and my daughters. What else did I know?

When he yawned, I knew my side of the conversation was stale. *He didn't take you to dinner to hear about your dead husband, seriously, Prissy.*

I switched gears, laughing at something he said that wasn't funny.

Our first date progressed from dread to okay, to more invitations and more accepting them. It wouldn't be long before I continued to date not only Joe the Legislator but also Don the Senator. He wore the same vest, drove the same car, and both called me "honey" and "darling."

I didn't like being anyone's darling or honey. I liked my own name.

CHAPTER THIRTY-FIVE

Dancing Widow

I WORE MY TIGHT jeans, halter top, and another pair of black stiletto heels I was trying to break in. People and stale smoke filled the Silver Slipper Lounge. It was Friday night in late April. Everyone was ready to end their week with drinks, cigarettes, music, and dancing. And here *I* was. In all my life, I had never been to a bar or lounge—nunca, never. Not even one of those bars off the lobby of a nice hotel. I always wanted to. On vacations or at conferences I'd attended with Boone, I would hear music coming through walls or open doors of hotel bars, melodic lyrics of a singer or songwriter luring me in.

"Hey, let's go have a listen?" I'd say, grabbing his hand.

"In there? No way, we aren't going in there." He didn't drink and didn't want to be associated with any characters in the bar who did.

But here I was on another date with Joe, the same guy Carole had set me up with weeks earlier. He turned out to be fun and a good dancer, meeting my short-list criteria.

I was trying to drink my cosmopolitan martini, shag dance, yack, and visit with strangers on the dance floor all at the same time. I was like a chicken in a coop full of feed. I loved it—the variety of people from all walks of life: plumbers, roofers, electricians, all sharing the dance floor with lobbyists, legislatures, senators, and me. I felt like somebody else, a different version of myself. Hell, I *was* somebody else. I looked like the merry widow to anyone watching. Honestly, I didn't much care if everyone thought I looked happy. I was happy. It was a sobering truth. I had been through so much, but no one there would have known based on my blinding smile.

Boone had been dead and buried for thirteen months. I had lost him fourteen months before he actually died. For me, it had been a long twenty-seven months. The very day his malignant brain tumor was diagnosed, the man I married shut down, vacated, and I was left with someone else.

One of my best friends, Nancy, lost her husband, Jim, a young guy in his fifties, like Boone. From Jim's lung cancer diagnosis to his funeral was a short four months. Nancy hadn't even wrapped her head around his diagnosis or prognosis before he was already dead. It was horribly sad, shocking, and final. I told her she was blessed.

"Who wants a long goodbye if you have to watch suffering day in and day out?" I told her one day.

She wanted Jim to last longer because she didn't have enough time to say everything. I had too much time to say nothing. We agreed to disagree.

The guilt followed me. I spent months trying to save a man I knew couldn't be saved. The best physicians in the country told me so, over and over. Only a naked Boone, kneeling and begging, forced me to bring him home from Houston and the ongoing torture. I didn't stop, though. I hauled the treatment back and infused him in the comfort of our own home.

I should have listened, enjoyed his presence while he was still present. I should have shared his final year with his children, his most cherished assets. Instead, I brought home an incoherent, frail, near-death stranger, unable to utter even one comprehensible sentence. It still shames me.

I realized only later what a dying person really needs more than just being saved. They need to be loved, touched, held, and conversed with. Boone needed, wanted, to talk about dying and life after death. I didn't. I couldn't.

Time and again he would say, "Will you lie with me?"

I always had an excuse and did little holding, lying, or talking. It was just too hard for me. In my defense—another truth—I believed I had no time to waste as precious time ticked by. Only later, when it was too late, would I understand all the missed opportunities: listening to him, learning from him, and helping him accept his inevitable and impending death. My willing him to live, and my blind faith in miracles, sabotaged our remaining days, weeks, and months.

I just couldn't accept my inability to save at least one of the two men I loved. My beloved father, the other man I'd failed, had succumbed to metastatic brain cancer. I was no quitter. Only too late I realized it wasn't one of my best qualities.

All I knew, as I twirled in the middle of the dance floor, was that I just wanted to keep dancing. Life could change on a dime.

PART THREE

Just when the caterpillar thought the world
was over, it became a butterfly.
—*Unknown*

CHAPTER THIRTY-SIX

Broken Promises

IT WAS ONE OF those beautiful April days when the smell of confederate jasmine filled the air, the breeze collecting its scent and merging it with blooming magnolias and lavender.

When I opened my mailbox, I found a card buried with all the bills and junk mail that came on a daily basis. The handwriting was beautiful, not script, but a very neat print with an edge of cursive. The envelope addressed to me had a return address from a street in Indianapolis that I didn't immediately recognize, but somehow, I instinctively knew. As I slipped it out, I could see the card was one of those blank ones. The note had been typed, cut, and pasted in perfect symmetry inside the Hallmark condolence card.

I knew his words had been carefully selected before being inscribed and pasted to the inside of the card and sent through the mail into my life. He had waited over thirty years and wanted his wording perfect.

> April 9, 1999
> Dearest Prissy,
>
> I visited Tallahassee last weekend, and as I have done for thirty years, I asked our mutual friends about how you and your family were getting along. This time I was terribly saddened to learn about your

> recent tragedy and with this letter am forwarding my condolences.
>
> Nine years ago a similar event occurred in our family, and we have never gotten over it. However, take comfort in knowing that our friends have helped soothe our sorrow, and our memories continue to bring us peace. Prissy, as I have done for thirty years, I shall continue to wish you the best and now will also pray that your friends soothe your sorrow and your memories bring you peace.
>
> Forever and a Day,
> Dale K. Elrod

It had been months since I had received a sympathy card. Boone had been dead over a year, so I was surprised to find one in the mailbox. Stranger still, I had received it from someone whose heart I knew I had broken.

He and I had not spoken or communicated since my junior year of college. It was one of those college love stories that young age and lack of maturity couldn't sustain. We had the most important ingredient—love—but lacked the knowledge, wisdom, and patience to go with it. I did, anyway.

I first saw him in the fall of 1967. I was sitting in Ken's Barbecue in my hometown of Lake City, Florida, a small, quaint town that had a population of about 2,500 or 3,000 people.

My girlfriends and I had been at cheerleading practice and, like most teenagers, had gone for our heavy snack before heading home for dinner, phone chats, and homework. I was wearing my cheerleading uniform: a short white pleated skirt with a purple and gold "Go Tigers" sweater. I had polished my black and white oxford shoes the night before; they looked like new.

The class ring hanging on the chain around my neck belonged to my boyfriend who had graduated the previous spring. He was going to the University of Florida playing football. I used the term *playing* lightly, since he was mostly sitting on the bench. Still, I liked to tell people he was a football player.

We had started dating when I was fifteen. He was two years older than me. We looked good together and were popular among our peers, making us a nauseating couple to some, I supposed.

He was a big, handsome guy, muscular, with dark brown eyes that matched his dark brown hair. His family was Mormon and practiced it diligently, which protected my virginity. He would be leaving soon to go to South America for his required church mission work. I guess his faith, coupled with my Catholic upbringing, was a bit unorthodox for a steady couple. Yet we had been together for over three years.

But as I sat thronged together with my friends at Ken's, I was mesmerized by a boy with sandy-blond hair across the restaurant. He was deep in conversation with his friend and barely glanced our way.

"Who are those guys by the window?" I asked my girlfriends. "Wait a second, then turn around and see."

My asking them not to turn around made them turn faster. It was like a perfectly choreographed movement, heads turning in unison. In our little town, everyone knew everyone. A new boy or boys in town were a conspicuous presence.

I announced I would find out who they were. I slid from the brown vinyl booth and walked over to their table with an air of sophistication I thought I had but probably didn't. I evaluated their looks, clothes, shoes, fingernails, and mannerisms in one quick sweep and began my introduction.

"Are you guys from the junior college?"

"Yeah," said the one with dark hair, not the blond I'd been eyeing.

Hanging from my neck, my boyfriend's ring glistened in the sunlight spilling through the restaurant's window.

"Hi, my name's Prissy." I pointed over to my friends. "We're sitting over there. We were just wondering where y'all are from."

"Indianapolis," the friendly one spoke again.

"Really? How'd you find this place?" I was still trying to get one word from the shy one.

Finally, he looked up from his plate of barbecue—an *enormous* plate of barbecue. His eyes were the most beautiful blue I'd ever seen. They were sparkling and translucent, intense, quiet, but telling. I'd heard the expression "Eyes are the windows to the soul." His soul was good . . . I could see it.

We talked a little more small talk, and I offered to give them my phone number, since they were new in town. After all, it was my town and *nobody* knew it better than me.

I scribbled my number on a napkin speckled with barbecue sauce. Both hands came up at once; I chose blue eyes. I'm not sure what I thought I was doing, really. I had a boyfriend, a serious boyfriend, as they would say. He was good-looking, played football (well—in theory), planned to be a lawyer, etc. He talked about getting married once we were out of college. He had been hanging around my home and family for over three years. Yet here I was, giving my phone number to some strange guy I knew nothing about and suggesting he call me.

He did. We began dating after a long-drawn-out breakup with my Mormon boyfriend involving unkind accusations, insensitive feelings, and teenage tears. Friends and family asked why I had become disillusioned so suddenly and discarded such a fine young man. I told them I just knew he wasn't right for me that very day in Ken's Barbecue. He wasn't my destiny. I met someone who I believed was.

I read the sympathy note again. I knew more about Dale than he realized. Even though I hadn't been in contact with him for over three decades, we had mutual friends. Every few years, I'd hear about his goings-on through one of them. In particular, Chip, one of Dale's oldest friends and the same guy from Ken's Barbecue, loved boasting about Dale's world travels, his accomplishments, and the financial success he had achieved. Every time Chip ran into me, he never failed to mention Dale's marital status—*single*, a confirmed bachelor all his life.

"I don't understand why he never married. What's the deal?" I asked Chip once. He was Dale's age about then, into his late forties.

"Honey, he never got over you. Don't you know that?"

I was shocked, maybe flattered in some sick way. Mostly, I questioned why.

Dale had once asked me to marry him.

"Ask me later," I'd said.

Marriage was the furthest thing from my mind. I wasn't even twenty yet and was enjoying my carefree life: school, friends, and college adventure. Plus, my strict father had preached the value of education my entire life.

"Don't talk marriage to me, not until you finish college," he lectured my sisters and me. "You better not get pregnant either."

I was mortified. My father was a small-town doctor, and I supposed he was seeing one pregnant teenager after another, which probably fueled his fear about his own three daughters. But his lecturing sure as hell worked. I wouldn't think of doing anything that might impregnate me. Dale wanting to run off and elope wasn't an option either. I had no intention of ever disappointing my dad, especially since I was the pleaser—possessing the middle child's strongest personality trait.

Dale knew my daddy well, like the other young men who previously hung around my house before him. He showcased the utmost respect and perhaps a little fear around my dad, Dr. Landrum. After all, my father was six-feet-five-inches tall. His height alone intimidated those testosterone-toting young boys.

Lake City was a typical small town with several mom-and-pop shops and a few grocery stores and restaurants. It was popular in the mobile home manufacturing business, with several lots showcasing new trailers. Dale liked to drive to the lots on weekends, with little else to do in our small town. One day as we drove around, Dale spotted a plastic sign with large black lettering faded from the hot Florida sun that read "Prices Slashed." Dale pointed to the old sign in the overgrown, weeded lot, swerved his Chevrolet in, and parked.

"Let's go see what they've got," he said.

An undereducated, commission-only salesman pounced on us the minute we got out of Dale's car.

"Come on in. We got what you lovebirds been looking for."

The man's forced smile bared uneven yellow teeth sandwiched between his paper-thin lips. One puff still remained on the Camel cigarette dangling from his stained fingers.

We walked through each trailer that was on display; they all featured the same dull, muted beige color scheme and country décor. The flammable fabrics, with their pungent odor, burned my nose. I tried to imagine myself living in one; I knew I never could.

In my heart it seemed romantic, grown-up, and almost like a fairy tale. My head felt different, though. I was living in a lovely split-level house with two housekeepers, a gardener, and a father who indulged all three of his daughters. Dale and the salesman should have shown me some double-wides, though I'm pretty certain seeing one even double the size could never have sealed that purchase.

Poor Dale had no money and lived in a trailer himself, the kind he pulled behind his car. It was turquoise striped, way small, with an itty-bitty bedroom that held, well, only a bed. The bathroom accommodated only the skinniest of folk. But, I once joked, if he wanted, he could pee and bathe at the same time.

He had remodeled the old thing, adding new carpeting, a new toilet, and the tiny shower. The walls of the one-hundred-square-foot trailer were covered with fake dark-wood paneling. I spruced it up by making him pleated curtains. He paid twenty-five dollars a month for hookup at Opal Jett's Trailer Park. Opal was one of my dad's patients. When Dale and I wanted to make out, we'd cruise into the trailer lot with his car lights off. I was petrified Opal might tell my dad I had been there, in Dale's trailer. Did I say my dad was strict? Um, yes, he was.

To me, Dale was just plain cool. He hailed from a big city—Indianapolis—had his own place (even if it was a camper trailer), drove a shiny red 1957 Chevrolet, smoked Pall Mall cigarettes, and went to the junior college. I was in high school and felt older just being associated with him.

He was the whole package and exuded a rebel appeal. He was smart, quiet, gymnast-lean, and kind to my younger sister, Gina. She told me none of my other boyfriends had been kind to her.

It was our third year of dating, my junior year of college about to start, when he suggested we transfer to the University of West Florida in Pensacola, where computer science was offered. He was a math whiz, and FSU had no computer science program at the time.

"Come with me to West Florida. We'll get married, and you can finish school there," he suggested.

Dale had become more studious, focused, and very motivated. He was tired of being poor and was ready to seek out his future and make some money. Two years younger, I still wanted to have fun and savor college life in my new and larger town, Tallahassee.

We rode over to Pensacola, and I looked at the school with him. But I knew I wouldn't go to such a small school in another small town. I'd spent long enough living in a small town, going to a small school. I wanted big, period.

I stayed at Florida State, pledged a sorority, and began to enjoy my last two years of college life. We agreed to see each other whenever we could on the weekends. It never happened. Once Dale pulled the stake and dragged his camper to Pensacola, our love affair ended. We just didn't know it yet.

A serious boyfriend was no longer on my agenda. I was too busy dating nonserious fraternity boys and decorating homecoming floats. I never answered Dale's letters or calls again. I was a coward and vanished from his life with no explanation at all. A few months later, I met Boone.

I slid the sympathy card back into the envelope and waited a few days before I wrote him back. I bought some plain pink stationery and a new pen. It was the first time I had written his name in over thirty years. It felt surreal.

April 18, 1999
Dear Dale,

I received your note the other day and was deeply touched. I must say I have received hundreds of notes and yours was truly from the heart. As hearts go . . . yes, mine was broken, but I am on the other side of the battlefield, I believe. I have learned life is what you make of it, and I have chosen to make the most of mine. I have two beautiful daughters and was adored for twenty-five years, so, what more could I want?

I've often wondered what the kaleidoscope of life has been for you, whether you achieved all of your dreams. My hope is that you have.

I am assuming you pursued your computer plans, and it was, no doubt, a very good decision. It is the world we now live, as you well know.

After Boone's death, I decided to change course and have gone to work full time for our governor, Jeb Bush. It is very interesting but a definite life change. My friends, of course, think I have lost my mind to start a career now. However, it is really fun for me. I'm working as an executive administrator to the general counsel for Jeb, so you really do meet some "whacks."

I would love to hear from you and am sorry I missed your visit to Tallahassee. I know you had a good time in this great city and look forward to seeing you next time.

Thanks again for your endearing note.

Fondly,
Prissy

I held on to my stamped letter two more days. Finally, I slid it into the mailbox and drove to work.

CHAPTER THIRTY-SEVEN

Words Unspoken

THE GIRLS AND I were meeting Du and Sallie for lunch at a brand-new Southern restaurant with all-you-can-eat country cooking. Not counting the wedding, it had been several months since the five of us had gathered. I let Du and Sallie choose the spot, certain they and the girls wouldn't fancy any place I preferred, as it might be healthier.

Sallie was busy working for a new family: a young couple with two small children. The mother was under Sallie's care after an undiagnosed sinus infection resulted in a catastrophic brain infection. Subsequently, she was left blind and deaf—a modern-day Helen Keller—with two small children and a husband away at work all day. My friend Gayle had matched Sallie and the young mother together after the tragedy occurred.

Sallie shared the challenges with us, such as how she was teaching the mother to communicate. Sallie came up with the idea of showing the woman how to spell words in the palm of Sallie's hand. I felt proud, as though Sallie were my child and I was her momma. It was clear she had found a new family she loved and worried about.

Du was still at the hospital, rolling his cart from room to room in his capacity as a lab technician. He was spending his nights sitting with an elder gentleman who had recently lost his wife, keeping him company and helping with all his personal needs.

"Christy, you see some men folk yet?" Sallie started in on me as soon as I sat down with my plate piled high from too many buffet choices. Du was laughing at her question, his mouth full of collard greens.

"Oh yeah, she's seeing them all right," Garrett said, rolling her eyes and picking at a chicken wing. "You wouldn't believe it, Sallie. She goes out every dang night with the same guy, who knows where." She was talking about Joe, the man I occasionally dated.

"You don't like him?" Du asked Garrett, having worked his way to his sweet potatoes. Everyone seemed to be ignoring the fact that I was sitting right there.

"I like him," Sara Britton volunteered. "I think he's nice. Garrett wouldn't like anybody she went out with."

"Um-hum, you're right, Sara. You're right about that," Sallie said.

It was true. Garrett had been more than a pill about my new persona: dating mother.

I decided to change the subject, since I was tired of them all having their fun at my expense. "Well, since I have you all here, I'll tell you some news."

Sallie was about to get up and head to the dessert table, but she sat back down.

"I got a letter from an old boyfriend," I said. Yep, I had their attention now, and no one was talking around me.

"Who? What's his name?" Garrett was the first with her line of interrogation.

I told them about the sympathy card and what little I knew about Dale, the boy I once knew.

"Where does he live?" Sallie asked next.

"Indianapolis, but I met him when he lived in Lake City."

Sara Britton was next. "How long did you date, Mom?"

"Three years."

"Why'd you break up?" Garrett asked.

"He wanted to go to a different school. I wanted to stay at FSU."

They asked more questions: Is he divorced or widowed? Does he have kids? What does he do? Their questions monopolized the next thirty minutes until I assured them I would find out everything they wanted to know. Garrett was smiling, probably because he lived a thousand miles away.

As we were about to leave, I asked Du about Willie Stokes. I'd been wondering if he still lived at the shelter, or rather, I *worried* he still lived at the shelter.

"Oh, Christy, you ain't heard?"

"Heard what?" I asked.

"He's dead. Was shot by some young punk trying to steal an old woman's purse. Willie, he tried get it back for her, and that boy shot him right in the heart."

I sensed my food rising from my full stomach and felt sick.

Later, I tried to make sense of it. I couldn't. I remembered hearing background news one evening, months earlier, paying no attention to the specifics. It was just another story about a robbery, knifing, or shooting around Martin Luther King Street. There was no mention of a courageous man who sacrificed his life for a frail and aged woman who clung to her purse. Or, that the hero was gentle and quiet, a man of few words who cared for others with grace and dignity. They never said he had a hard life, which forced him to live with practically nothing for most of his life.

I wondered if the story would have been told differently had he been a white man shot while trying to retrieve a purse from a robber. I knew the answer; of course it would.

To others, Willie Stokes may have been some nobody, with no importance or fame, just some homeless man. But to me, my girls, and Boone, well, he was somebody. He mattered. My heart ached that he died without my ever telling him so.

CHAPTER THIRTY-EIGHT

ESFJ

THE ENVELOPE LIKELY CONTAINING my personality assessment results had arrived in the mail two days earlier. I tucked the still unopened envelope in my beach bag just before heading to my beach house in St. Teresa for a weekend of solitude. It had been an endless, boring week at work. I looked forward to the mystery novel nestled inside the bag, along with my delicious bottle of wine.

The Myers-Briggs Type Indicator, or MBTI, is a standardized test that assesses personality type. It had recently been administered to Garrett as a requirement for her job. I took the test for fun after she and Gayle suggested *everyone* should know their personality type.

After unpacking the few groceries I bought and slipping fresh sheets on the bed, I poured my wine and headed for my deck chair awaiting me outside overlooking the water's edge. I joined the other guests—two lone seagulls—perched on the railing. Growing up in Florida, I had learned that male and female seagulls mated for life. I envied them.

It was peaceful, since few people had arrived for the weekend yet. I inhaled sea air and listened to children's laughter as they skidded across the sands of low tide. Finally, I pulled out the envelope with the results from the Myers-Briggs people, took another sip of wine, and opened the envelope. I skipped the boring part, which seemed to be most of it, looking for the final evaluation that rested in the closing paragraph. There it was: ESFJ (Extraversion, Sensing, Feeling, and Judging).

According to experts—who they were is debatable—I had a particular quality. "ESFJs need to rescue the perishing people, believing that if enough time, enough energy, and caring is given, anyone can be saved . . . "

There it was, in black and white, for me and anyone else to see. The warm Florida sun cast its glow on my MBTI evaluation like a big ol' spotlight. It justified all the mistakes I made, all the guilt that consumed me. I'd had to try and save Boone. Of course I had. It was in my DNA. It explained who I was and who I had become because of who I was. I know such a statement made no sense to anyone else, but it made perfect sense to me. I thanked God and the test evaluator for that profound revelation.

Captivated by a breathtaking breeze and swaying sea oats, I closed my eyes, and with credence, I believed Boone understood, tolerated, and accepted my manic behavior. Despite the warm temperature and the cloudless sky, I felt my goose bumps then a chill. For the first time since his death, I believed Boone forgave me, or maybe I just forgave myself. Either way, it didn't matter. On a picturesque May afternoon, I felt changed, somehow redeemed. I even felt happy, almost like the Prissy before, the one who enjoyed a Pollyanna personality, which I had just learned had its own professional description as well: ESFJ.

Two days later, I closed up the beach house and drove the forty-five minutes back home with my Jeep windows down and the country music blaring, feeling ten years younger. I drove back to Tallahassee as someone new.

CHAPTER THIRTY-NINE

I've Got Mail

HOME FROM THE BEACH, I went through the mail and found another letter from Dale. This time it was longer—two pages. He inquired about my entire family: my mother and sisters, my children, and Mazelle. He wrote about his family, whom I remembered, having spent a week with them back when I was in high school and dating Dale. I learned he had worked in different parts of the world and lived in some exciting places. Once an engineer, he changed courses later in life, studied mergers and acquisitions, and started buying businesses. He wrote,

> My new path has been a great growing experience for me. It has tamed my ego, and helped me develop greater patience and humility, provided me with more confidence, and enhanced my relationships with family and friends.

I liked what he said, this boy, now man. But it was his closing paragraph that kept me interested.

> Prissy, while you were a wife and mother, I secretly wished you the best. Now that your life has changed, I openly wish you the best and I also hope your new path is strewn with pleasure.

Secretly and *openly*. I wondered what he meant by those two words. I waited five days then wrote him back. I answered all his questions and filled in a short version of my life. In closing, I suggested we e-mail rather than exchange postal letters and shared my e-mail address with him. In truth, I was crazy busy and didn't seem to have five minutes to sit down and write a long paper letter back. It was the end of the legislative session, and I was in overload. Sara Britton was graduating from high school, and Garrett was graduating from FSU business school and trying to get into law school. Let's not forget, I was still going out nights with both sides of the legislative body: one senator and one legislator. Still, I sure did like Dale's way with words and looked forward to his reply.

An e-mail came a few days later with subject "Belly Laughs & Jewels." He called my daughters "jewels" and enjoyed my style of writing. Two compliments in one short page. I replied, and our e-mail relationship began.

Our back-and-forth e-mails were friendly, chatty, and funny. Still, I wasted no time in asking,

> I am curious—you have no children of your own? Did you ever marry? If not, why? You would have been a great husband and father. If you find someone young enough, you can still have a family. Believe it or not, there are plenty of my friends (guys, of course) who ran off with their "sexataries" and started a new family in their 50s.

I was fishing. I remembered my conversation with Chip and his story of how Dale never got over me.

Dale replied the next day:

> My brother and I have over 100 employees, and the only sexataries we have in our company are 450 MHz Dells. I have never married, was close twice. Once, she thought the timing was not right; the other, well, I decided the time would never be right.

> Being alone has good points and bad points, being married I imagine is probably the same. I think we humans need the good from both and that is what I am looking for. It is hard to find, but good things always are.

It was a good answer, but not to my question. By then it had been four weeks since I received his sympathy card. His next e-mail took me by surprise. He wrote,

> I have this cardboard box heaping full of pictures and other things I have saved over the years. I call this my memory box. After you responded to my sympathy card, I dug thirty years deep into my box to refresh my memory.

He had scanned a picture of me standing on the beach. I was wearing a flannel shirt I had given him, grinning into the camera. I remembered he had taken me to Daytona Beach for my first camping trip. It was windy and cold in the middle of a Florida winter. He had saved the picture of me for thirty years.

I read more of his e-mail and learned he still had the same amount of hair, though it had turned colors, now gray and brown, the gray battling for dominance. And he had a beard. He wrote,

> If you like, one of these days we will meet and see for ourselves what has happened to our looks over the last 30 years. To me, the less we both know about how each of us looks now, the more fun and exciting that moment will be. At 51, I cherish the exciting moments in my life and sometimes the less I know the more excited I become. However, if you don't agree, I will be happy to take a picture, digitize it, and e-mail it to you.

Somehow, it was then that I decided the fun was in the mystery. I printed the scanned picture from the computer, slid it into my desk drawer, and tapped my reply.

> You are right. I would rather just imagine and forget the digital pictures. That would take all the fun out of it. One day we will meet somewhere between Tallahassee and Indianapolis and try and find each other in a crowd. You may have to lose the beard, since that would give it away.

I looked forward to coming home from work and checking my e-mails. I had recently remodeled the master bedroom, tearing down the wall between the guest room, where Boone died, and the master bedroom and designing a master suite with a sitting area and office combination. It was decorated French style, very feminine, a perfect place to manage my new life.

The girls came for dinner, and I was in my office reading my latest e-mail when Sara Britton walked in and flopped down on the chaise lounge next to my desk.

"Are you still writing that guy?"

"What guy?"

"You know what guy, Mom."

"Maybe I am."

"God, you've been writing him over a month. What are you saying?"

"I'm telling him what a pain in the ass you are, how I have no privacy." I laughed, shutting my laptop.

During dinner, she and Garrett both grilled me.

"Is he coming to town?" Sara Britton asked.

"We're just friends." I reached for the butter. "We have no plans to meet. He's my pen pal."

"You mean a cybersex pal," Garrett said, and both girls laughed out loud.

After they left, I cleaned up, poured a glass of wine, and slipped back into my retreat to check my in-box. I had AOL as my e-mail server at the time and loved to hear the three words: "You've got mail." I did and opened it.

> Finding each other in a crowd, that's a better twist than mine and sounds exciting. I have thought about it, and I cannot remember your voice. I think not remembering what you sound like will cause me to imagine even more. If you don't remember the sound of mine, maybe you think we should just imagine that too.

It was then that I decided no phone calls either. We wouldn't share any pictures or talk on the phone. We would exchange e-mails and learn who we had become. I finished reading his e-mail.

> Sometimes charming people lead charming lives. I remember you as very charming, and a charmed life for you sounds natural to me. Spoiled, I do not remember you that way, but at that time, I do remember wanting to. I like nice things too. I like dressing up and dressing down. I like to socialize throughout the spectrum, from the janitors to the Jebs, and I feel most comfortable with those that feel most comfortable with me. I do my own laundry and do not like to pinch pennies or spend a dollar to save one.

The boy who once pulled his living quarters behind a car still seemed like a nice guy. It was what drew me to him so many years ago. I left his e-mail unanswered and went to bed remembering.

CHAPTER FORTY

Two Boxes

IT WAS THE END of May, and Dale and I were still writing. By then, I had been working for four months. The first two months had kept me busy learning the political world, and the following two months I was ensconced in the whole legislative process. Time flew, since it was both challenging and fun. Governing law ran through the historical corridors like an electrical current. But now that the session had adjourned and all the movers and shakers left town, those same corridors were empty, lonely, and my new career became boring.

I filled the boredom by becoming a gym rat. Nancy, my girlfriend, was my rat partner, and we hired a trainer, Mary Barley, to whip us into shape. She was our age and gorgeous. We wanted to look just like her but not work as hard and told her so. We had enrolled in Tae Bo classes and spent three evenings a week kicking and punching. My widowed body became cut, lean, and muscular, especially since I was still climbing the twenty-two flights of stairs every day.

My nights and weekends were filled with the new routine. I continued my fashion consulting business with Doncaster, selling the designer frocks on the side, and created as many other activities as I could to keep busy. Beverly was relieved to have me back in the clothing business; she had carried the burden alone from the day Boone was diagnosed.

Dale's e-mails became an added pleasure, and our communication every few days grew to every day and sometimes twice a day. I wrote to him like he was a girlfriend, even giving him narrative summaries of my dates: who he was, what he did, and where we ate. I told him stories about other people and things in my life and soon started telling others about him.

One day, about two months into our everyday writing, I wrote,

> Do you remember my 18th birthday when we went to an antique show at the National Guard Armory in Lake City? You bought me this old hair accessory box that was very French looking. Inside there was an ivory hairbrush, comb, mirror, mustache brush, and other gizmos. It is still sitting on my dressing table after thirty years. It was very old when you bought it, unsure of the date, but now it is really old and quite beautiful, very unusual. I thought you would like to know it was a very good investment on your part.

I had more I wanted say. I was careful how I phrased my next question, still remembering my conversation with Chip, aware I *must* have hurt Dale. I knew I had behaved badly but couldn't remember how badly.

> I was trying to figure out when we actually broke up and why. Were you at a different school or still at FSU? Did we have a fight? I don't remember and I think that is very strange on my part. Was it mutual, or was it you, or was it me? It must have been a bad memory, so I erased it. I think God has given me a gift to allow me to do this with my mind. However, if I was wicked, I do want to know.

His reply came an hour later.

> I had forgotten all about that box until you reminded me. After reading about it, I remembered buying it for you. I can almost see it in my mind and am happy you enjoyed it over the years. You were always interested in the finer things, even then. Now, let me please tell you my own box story. It is an oak box, held together with dovetail joints, with a hyperbolic cross-sectioned top, hinged with brass and marked with an engraved brass plate. The engraving on the brass plate is in script and reads "Prissy." You gave me this box for a birthday of mine, and I, too, still have it. It resides in my office on my bookshelf and, for as long as I can remember, always has. There are probably two years of pictures of you in my box. It is a strange feeling, once again, enjoying a gift from thirty years ago. I am thankful for having the chance to tell you how much I have enjoyed it for all those years.

Pictures of me in a box I gave him—*still.* I imagined how cocky I must have been to have *my* name engraved on top of *his* birthday gift. Surely, most normal people would have put the name of the recipient. I was embarrassed, but it was thirty years too late. I was still wondering why he hadn't replied to my question about our breakup when another e-mail popped up.

> As I remember, our previous relationship ended when our life paths split. At FSU, I was doing well as a math major, but suddenly discovered computers. I thought computers were my future. At that time, FSU offered no computer science courses. West Florida had a great computer science program and one of the few in the country. I applied and was accepted. I tried to talk you in to attending West Florida, but your interests were in Tallahassee and you had moved into an apartment with your sister. I left for Pensacola and we tried to stay in touch, and it didn't work out.

> There are other things I would like to say about the forgoing subject, including an apology or two. However, it is too easy to apologize on paper, therefore, I shall wait, and then I can look straight into your eyes to tell you for what I am sorry. Prissy, you were never wicked. God just had something else for us to do, and consequently, our time together ended.

Other things he wanted to apologize for. I had no idea what he meant or what he ever did to me. I was the one who left him even though I told him I couldn't remember. I knew what I had done. I wrote back.

> It's gratifying to know I was not one of those "wicked witch sisters" but remain Cinderella instead. I'm also glad to know you remembered the circumstances of the parting of our ways and to know it was mutual. However, you telling me you have two years of pictures… It's a long time to wait for me to hear some apology that I am now wondering about. Perhaps paper will have to do, or you need to be looking for that crowded place.

Wow, did I just hint we meet? I closed my computer, showered, dressed, and left to meet my daughters for lunch, thinking I might tell them a bit more about my old boyfriend, maybe over dessert.

CHAPTER FORTY-ONE

The Voice

THE GIRLS AND I met at Food Glorious Food for a festive lunch honoring Sara Britton's upcoming high school graduation. By the end of the week, she would officially be a high school graduate. We sat at our table for four, one chair painfully vacant. Not wanting to acknowledge Boone's absence and sadden our mood, I started bringing them up to date on Dale and our e-mailing saga. That reminded Sara Britton of something that had happened a few years earlier, and she'd forgotten to tell me.

"Mom, you won't believe this. Remember about three years ago, it was a school night, you came in my room and told me to get off the phone?"

"You're kidding, right? I can hardly remember what happened yesterday, so three years is a stretch, Sara Britton," I said, laughing.

"No, listen. I remembered talking to Jared Miller. He was in Indiana with his dad visiting some guy. Remember, I asked if you remembered a guy named Dale you used to date? That's where they were, his lake house. Jared was going on and on about four-wheelers, all the toys he had, his four hundred acres and seven miles of lakes. I was talking to Jared three years ago about somebody you're writing to now. That's so weird," she said.

I did remember as soon as she finished the story. But more than just remembering her story, I saw it as some kind of sign, though I didn't tell her so. I always looked for signs, as though my stars were always trying to align. I was also intrigued by the wealth that the boy who used to drive me around to trailer parks had accumulated. If it was true, I was happy for his success.

At the end of the long workweek, I bumped into Lyn, another good friend, at the grocery store. Her husband, Fred, had loaned me the American Express credit card I'd used in Houston.

"How's your summer?" I asked her.

"It's good. How's yours?"

"It's good. Still working at the capitol."

"Darn, I forgot. I was thinking about you yesterday, planning to call you and see if you wanted to go with some of us to England in July. Julie, Patti, Mary Ann, Linda, and me, we're staying in London a week and then heading to the country for antiquing. Guess you can't take off work, huh?"

"That sounds like a fun trip. I wish I could."

We talked some more, and I headed home in a different state of mind. I was envious, almost resentful, and I didn't like myself very much for it. Good friends, who had husbands, taking a girls' trip to Europe, and none of them had a care in the world. I wanted to be one of them.

When I got home, I sent Dale an e-mail. I mentioned my mood and asked,

> Why didn't you call me rather than send a sympathy card?

He responded immediately.

> I truly believe had I sent my condolences by telephone, you and I would not be communicating. I believe I am the world's worst telephone communicator; I'm no good at it. I still remember the first time hanging up and thinking, that was lame, real

> lame. I can't believe she agreed to see me. The point is I am glad you chose no phone calls between us. Maybe I still stand a chance. This social e-mail discovery has been good for me, and I will forever associate that good with you.

He also mentioned his friends Doug and Carole, who had asked him if he thought we'd ever meet each other again. It was thrown in at the end of his e-mail.

I answered him too quickly:

> Tell your friends what I told the few who know about us—hold their horses. What's a little longer when it has already been thirty years? And to answer their questions—why have we not talked on the phone, when, where, and why have we not planned to meet?—here are my answers:
>
> Why talk on the phone when creativity and thoughts are better put in writing?
>
> Perhaps in July.
>
> To be determined.
>
> Because it will be so incredibly weird to see you after all these years.

Dale's response came just as fast, as though he was staring at his computer and waiting for my e-mail.

> Your response to Doug and Carole shook me to the core. I am not sure I can get ready by July: my liposuction, face-lift, diet, and wardrobe, plus shave my beard and dye my hair. I would say my problem with our reunion won't be its weirdness but rather the calming of my nerves. Prissy, I am 51 years old and I don't understand why I am nervous about meeting you again.

Our e-mails went back and forth that Friday evening. So many, I forgot I was feeling sorry for myself about not joining my friends for the trip to Europe. I replied to his concerns, fears, and trepidation about our meeting.

> You are so silly. If it makes you nervous, then we shall never meet. Then you will need no liposuction, dye, clothes, or anything else. You may be just as happy e-mailing forever. I can't say the same for Doug and Carole though. We can decide later how best to handle you. It's strange, but I seem fine with it and not the least bit nervous or apprehensive. Nothing is written in stone, so, relax.

Dale had become my sounding board over the last few weeks. I started sharing things with him I wasn't sharing with anyone else in my life. More afraid than anyone knew, I felt safe with this boy from my youth. He was smart, a successful businessman, and running a company. He also gave good advice on anything and everything I asked.

Being the trustee of my father's estate and Boone's—now mine—was a huge responsibility for someone who was only one year in the grieving cycle. Some decisions were conflicting and difficult to make. I was trying to sell real estate for my mother and manage her assets. My fiduciary responsibilities were twofold: I had to think about me and my girls, plus my mother and my sisters. Dale was a good advisor.

I told him about my friends going to Europe and how I envied them. I had mentioned to him in earlier e-mails that I was growing bored with my job.

> You thought I was just kidding when I said I was going to quit my job and go to Tuscany. Funny thing. I was kidding, but something happened to me today. I can't explain it, even to myself, but I really am thinking of quitting and taking off to travel

> for a while. Is that a dumb, irresponsible, immature, wasteful thing to do?

What? How could I quit the job I only just started? I was mortified for even thinking it. But yet . . . I so wanted to. I shut down the computer and went to bed ashamed of myself.

The next day was Sara Britton's graduation ceremony. She was sad, missing her daddy on the first big occasion of her life without him. I wrote to Dale and shared her pain, thinking he might somehow understand. Then I told him the thoughts that had been rattling in my head.

> I didn't sleep last night. Maybe it has something to do with wanting to change my course in life yet again. My sisters say I went to work because I wanted to show the world I could live on my own and not spend any of Boone's money he worked for all those years, suggesting I felt guilty spending what he never would. Maybe they're right. I really don't know what I'm trying to prove. I'm totally exhausted in my journey to prove to everyone how superwoman I am. Since the day Boone was diagnosed, I have not been away from responsibility. I want to be carefree and leave all this behind, get away from all the people, places, and things and just heal from the inside. So, it may not be Tuscany, but I'm going to quit my job I was so graciously given. You are probably still catatonic over the July thing. We can move our meeting to fall if you like. I decided to put the ball entirely in your court. Remember, I am casting away all responsibility as of today. Now you must decide the when and where and make all the arrangements.

I wanted to leave my job but still felt conflicted, and I especially worried about quitting on Frank and letting him down. I was no quitter, I reminded myself again. But yet, here I was entertaining doing just that.

As I sat at Sara Britton's graduation, I was rethinking my decision when I read the back of the program handed to me. I couldn't believe it. It was "The Voice," a poem written by Shel Silverstein, whose books I had read over and over to my girls when they were young. The poem was about listening to the voice inside your head and how only you could decide what was best for yourself.

I believed it was just another sign. My baby girl graduated from high school the same night I decided to quit my job. It was perfect, all thanks to Mr. Silverstein.

CHAPTER FORTY-TWO

Bedazzled

YEARS EARLIER, LONG BEFORE reconnecting with Dale, I recalled reading an article that said the sight, sound, or even smell of a first love seems to burrow deep into the brain. If there are strong emotional attachments in late adolescence and early adulthood, they are marked like Post-it notes in our memories. Maybe that was why I found myself revisiting the past, and it explained why I still felt so comfortable and connected to Dale, though I had no idea what he looked like, or even sounded like, after ten weeks of writing. I pictured a blond-haired, blue-eyed, skinny, twentysomething boy writing to me, even though it had been three decades. My vision of him made me feel younger too.

The day after Sara Britton's graduation, a Sunday, I was trying to figure out exactly what I could say to Frank now that I had decided to quit. Never one to procrastinate, I wanted to tell him the next day but was considering sending a letter of resignation by e-mail. *Could I get any more unprofessional?* I wondered. I poured my morning coffee and headed to my desk to draft the "I quit" letter and found a new message from Dale.

> Your heart will always tell you what to do; your mind will only screw it up. Worry about yourself, and everyone else will be well because you are. I think your new plan comes from your heart, and if that is true, then don't let your mind change. Too

> much responsibility is not healthy, and that comes from someone who knows. That is one of the reasons why I am trying to change my path too. Life is too short, enjoy it while you can. Regarding our meeting, I do not want to put it off. I want to meet you again, look in your eyes, and have a chance to know you more. Our e-mails have been revealing, but now I would like to talk about all the things that have been hidden between our lines. I gladly accept this responsibility. I will decide when and where, you should not worry about anything. I will make all the arrangements, please trust me, as I am what I have written.

He understood why I wanted to quit and wasn't judging me. He didn't think me irresponsible or a defeatist. This guy was too good to be true. *Wait . . . did he write we're going to meet?* I reread his e-mail again. I froze. Holy cow . . . he did say it, and he was going to plan the whole thing. I would ask him more about that later. First, I had to write the dang letter to Frank and needed advice.

> You have probably had many folks quit on you over the years. How should I approach it? I am thinking of e-mailing Frank from home today. What do you think?

It was early Sunday evening before I checked my e-mails again, and his response to my question awaited.

> I would write him a nice resignation letter. I would write the letter one day, set it aside until the next day. I would reread it, and then if necessary, I would edit/rewrite it. I would keep the letter to a length of less than one page. I would be truthful about my life struggle and ask him for his understanding. I would inform him you are giving a longer than normal notice as you respect him so. I would

> not disturb him on Sunday. Early this week, I would give him the letter through the normal channel; make it a hardcopy, no e-mail, no verbal. Emotionally prepare yourself for the post-resignation blues. As long as this is from your heart, you will be okay. Remember, "breaking up is hard to do."

I laughed out loud. Clearly, this man didn't know me at all. His long, professional recommendation would made perfect sense to a sensible one. That wasn't me. I had already sent my resignation to Frank—on *Sunday*, by *e-mail*—and quit. There was no hardcopy either.

> Had I gotten your good advice, I would have listened—maybe. Yours was much more professional. However, I've determined I'm not too professional and felt like a duck out of water. I think I am going to London with friends in July, so when you decide the where, I think the when will have to be chosen by both of us.

I picked up the phone and called Lyn to tell her I was going to Europe with my girlfriends after all.

On Monday morning, I didn't feel quite as confident as I had Sunday night. I found the same spot in the garage where I had parked over the last six months, gathered my things, and walked toward the capitol building.

I was embarrassed and worried over what waited for me. I wasn't even sure Frank received my e-mail, especially since he never responded. I crossed Monroe Street and climbed the hill toward the capitol, breathing deeply as the morning sun bounced its glare off the passing cars. My nerves were as edgy as the day I first met Frank, the day he offered me the job. I had quit. There was that word again, messing with my mind, conflicting my already-made decision.

Late that afternoon, I came home relieved, feeling a weight was lifted. I kicked off my heels and turned on my laptop, excited to write.

> Things went great. Frank was the best, a true friend, a genuinely nice guy. He said screw the job, do what I needed to. Told me he would beg me to stay but cared too much for me to do that. He was relieved I wasn't quitting the job to run off with one of those legislators, even gave me advice on not being taken advantage of by some of them. Oh yes, I apologized for the unprofessional e-mail. He said it was just perfect—so like me. So, now the planning begins.

I had dinner with Sara Britton and Garrett, told them I had turned in my resignation, and informed them Dale and I were planning on meeting. Sara Britton was excited, always one for an adventure; Garrett, not so much. Dale was no threat to her a thousand miles away, but he should stay there as far as she was concerned. Dale was a pen pal for her mother, but she didn't know him from Adam, and frankly, didn't want to. I drove home less enthused about our reunion than when I had arrived. Another e-mail awaited and changed my mood.

> You can't know where we go, you were right, as the shedding of all responsibility comes with a big price—mystery. I am planning our meeting for the weekend of July 16–18. Today I will begin to put it together, and if that isn't okay, let me know. I have a good plan but must work out all of the details, as the crowd must be just right.

Geez, he really was taking charge. I was meeting him. There was no tease anymore. I wasn't sure how to share my next thought but had to make sure he knew.

> The date is fine, but remember, "I'm not that kind of girl," so separate rooms please.

What a presumptuous statement—what was I thinking? Embarrassed, I wanted to retrieve it, but it was too late, so I waited for his reply. It came far too soon.

> Regarding your room request, you never were that kind of girl. And I hope you remember I never was that kind of guy. As the planner of this gathering, I guarantee you that the person you pick out of that crowd shall be a perfect gentleman. As I said, no need to worry; you knew me then and have read about me now. Trust me. My soul has not changed.

I loved how he wrote and continued reading.

> I was worried for a while, but now that I have my plan, my nervousness has turned into excitement. I may have another case of the nervous knees when we actually meet. This little plan of mine should be fun. It will keep you guessing all the way to the crowd. It will be great to see you again, Priscilla Monica, and getting us to the crowd where I shall find you will be my pleasure.

I was bedazzled.

CHAPTER FORTY-THREE

Clueless

THE SUMMER DAYS PASSED quickly, though the heat and humidity of the Florida sun remained stagnant. Frank, the deputy general counselor, shared my resignation news with his boss, the general counselor. I was nervous when she called me into her office on Wednesday afternoon, afraid she would reprimand me for my quick turnaround and abrupt departure.

It was the exact opposite. She was ingratiating and told me a job would be waiting for me anytime I wanted. I thanked her with a handshake and assured her I would remain until my replacement was found. Afterward, I felt confident I'd made the right decision no matter how impromptu it was.

I had dinner plans with my good friends Gayle and Nancy after work. I decided to share my Europe plans with them, along with the Dale e-mails and us reuniting. I wanted to see how they would respond compared to Garrett.

"Prissy, something must be wrong with him. He never married. Why is that? That's just weird to me. Are you sure he's not gay?" Gayle began her summation of everything she had been holding back. She continued, "What do you even know about him? What if he dresses funny?"

"You're kidding, right?" I told her, shaking my head in disbelief. "I have no idea how he dresses and could care less. That's about as superficial as you can get, and no, he's not gay."

"I don't know about this. You don't even know what he looks like, could be some fat old guy. I'm not judging, but I'd want to know what somebody looked like before I spent a whole weekend with him. Can he scan a picture to you?" Nancy asked.

"I don't want him to scan a picture. We're not exchanging any pictures—that's the fun. We're picking each other out of a crowd."

"Have you talked to him on the phone? How does he sound?" Gayle asked.

"We're not talking on the phone either. We're just e-mailing."

"Why aren't you talking on the phone? What does that have to do with not sending pictures?" Nancy asked after ordering our second bottle of wine. I knew I would need it from the way our conversation was headed.

"Look, I know it sounds crazy. It does. I get that. But it is so much fun reading his e-mails. I'm getting to know him from the inside, just the opposite of anyone else, everyone else, I would go out with. Think about it, really knowing someone *before* a first, blind date. It's perfect. Besides, I knew him before, so I'm getting to know him again. His looks are secondary. Who cares what he looks like at this point? I'm not marrying the guy. Relax, you two."

"You'll care if you get there and are stuck with some fat nerd you have to spend your whole weekend with," Nancy said, laughing, and Gayle joined in.

After two bottles of wine, I laughed too. But by the night's end, they had me worried, and the more I drank, the more shallow I became. I opened my laptop when I got home and drafted an e-mail.

> Do you still think it is a good idea? I do, but we should not set our expectations too high and then one is never disappointed. Now the game starts... Hints, please?

I went to bed worried, wondering, and having drunk too much wine.

The next morning I made coffee then went back and booted up my computer. His response awaited.

> Yes, without a doubt, I still think it is a good idea, and I wouldn't miss it for anything. As far as expectations go, I have one—I expect we both shall have a wonderful time, nothing more or less. Hints shall be forthcoming. I am thinking about how best to hint. Too much information could spoil it, but too little information could frighten you. I will think about this problem and get back to you.

Huh? Frighten me . . . ? What could he plan that would possibly frighten me? I left for work conjuring some unimaginable things, hoping a hint would come soon, knowing I could still change my mind.

When I got home after work, there was another e-mail. I read the subject line: "Hint Disbursement Rules." I laughed and realized he took our mystery meeting to a whole new level. I hated rules but read his e-mail with an open mind.

> I've now decided how to manage your hint requests. I'll provide a daily hint, each hint separately labeled, arriving as stand-alone e-mails, and all shall accumulate. I may or may not be able to answer your questions about them; however, you can ask. If you become worried, frightened, or displeased, please immediately interact. I know you elected me arranger. However, if I am no good at it, please tell me. The first week of hints are very important, and it won't be too late to accommodate your concerns. However, one week from now, it will be.

I had another e-mail and opened it.

> Subject: Thirty-year reunion (Hint 1)
>
> Our reunion shall be held somewhere between Tallahassee and Indianapolis. I think it is an unfamiliar place to both of us. Previously, we agreed to meet by picking one another out of a crowd. The crowd shall not be too big as to make it impossible to find one another, nor shall it be too small to make it mundane. We shall dress as the crowd we are mingling in dresses. The crowd shall be a pleasant and relaxing one; therefore, we shall not be meeting at the airport.

When I finished reading his rules and the very first hint, I had no clue where to start guessing. It told me nothing and was a ridiculous hint. It could be anywhere.

When I awoke the next morning, another hint awaited like an unwrapped present to be opened.

> Subject: Hint 2
>
> Even though you and I will not meet in the airport, when you deplane, you will recognize a friendly stockholder. He will be trustworthy and shall assist you and show you the way. You may not know this stockholder today, but it is certain you will before July 13.

I left the house for brunch completely baffled. Stockholder? To whom, of what? I didn't know this stockholder but would by July 13. Huh? Two hints that didn't help one bit in my figuring out where we were meeting. I knew it would be a long cyber treasure hunt at the pace I was going.

But I knew I had more important things to figure out as I drove to Food Glorious Food for Sunday brunch. I had two daughters waiting with their hearts still broken. It was Father's Day, a ceremonial day we had always celebrated full throttle. It was Boone's special day; but now, to Sara Britton and Garrett, it was a day celebrated by their friends with *their* fathers. They felt cheated. We all did, as we ordered omelets in awkward silence.

CHAPTER FORTY-FOUR

Green Flannel Shirt

THE NEXT MORNING, I found my next hint—number three—waiting on my computer. Clearly, the man never slept. I glanced at the time documented by my server—2:40 a.m. In one of his e-mails, Dale had said he was an early riser. Geez, I didn't realize he meant the middle of the night. I made a mental note to ask him about his habits then read his e-mail.

> Subject: Thirty-Year Reunion Hint 3
>
> The town of our meeting is near the water but not the beach. It lies somewhere in North America between the 30th and 40th parallels. I have never been there but will go there to make arrangements before you. It is not typically an unhappy place, but when we both leave, we could be carrying the blues.

What? Was he kidding me? I was horrible at geography and had no clue what parallels even were, much less meeting somewhere between them. I arrived at my office and decided to enlist my cubicle mate, Sandra, the once unfriendly girl who'd befriended me with chocolates and a smile. Together we could try and decipher his latest hint. Heck, I might even ask Frank, my boss, to help. After all, he graduated from Yale Law School, so surely he was proficient in geography.

Frank was out for the day; we located an atlas and searched but found nothing that helped. I still had no idea what it meant but decided to quit messing with it and actually do my job, the one I was being paid to do, especially since the days remaining were few and I wanted to leave a good last impression.

After lunch, Frank remained out of the office, so feeling restless, I opened my personal e-mail. Another message waited.

> Subject: Green flannel shirt
>
> Remember in one of my earlier e-mails, I told you I had kept something else you had given me, besides the box. I didn't tell you what it was and now I will. Remember the photo I held on to and scanned to you? You were wearing a green and white heavy flannel shirt, standing on the beach. It was cold that day, so I had given you the one I was wearing. Actually, the shirt was a birthday gift from you to me. Prissy, to this day, I continue to possess it. It fits me and it looks like you gave it to me just last year. In the fall of each year, I enjoy taking walks in my forest and wear your shirt. Your gift is just right—not too heavy and not too light. Over the years, for forest walks, I have worn that shirt fifty times at least. For each of those forest walks, as I would take my first few steps, I would always fondly think and wonder about you. Prissy, now you know all about another one of your gifts to me—my green flannel shirt.

I signed out without responding. I was worried. He still had pictures, gifts, and now a piece of clothing—after thirty years. *What had I done to him?* I wondered. This boy, now man, held on to insignificant pieces, reminders, as if they were treasures. I should have been flattered. I was anything but. I had the urge to share this news with someone else but certainly not either of my daughters. I called my sister Deborah and read the e-mail to her.

"Geez, you better think twice before you meet him again. Think about it. You could mess him up more if you don't like him after all this," she offered.

Her advice made sense. It did, but I ignored it. I wanted to see him again. I was drawn to him and admired his writing, words, and wisdom. I moved forward, despite his revealing, heartfelt e-mails. I decided to play our communication more platonically, not wanting to lead him on more than I already had.

I went back to writing about other men I was dating, hoping it would keep a distance between us, besides the thousand miles. I didn't want to be responsible for wreaking sadness on him should our imminent reunion be disappointing to me.

I knew in my heart he didn't want to hear about the concert, dinner, or wedding I'd attended with someone else. Uninterested in any of them romantically myself, I wrote about them anyway. I became protective of Dale, having realized what I did to him as a girl and worried what I might do to him now, as a woman.

He ignored my mentioning of others and continued with the mystery game. We were only weeks until our reuniting, and I still had no idea where I was meeting him.

> Subject: Thirty-Year Reunion Hint 4
>
> After we meet we can choose to enjoy the unique nightlife or not, whichever we prefer. This city was named after one south of Cairo, but while there, you won't feel like you're in any kind of danger. The city was named by a famous long-haired man on a twenty.

He was the worst hinter, or the best, depending on who was playing the game. I was ready to finish it, though, and know where I was going.

I joined girlfriends for dinner. We drank too much wine and spent the evening conjuring all the places he might be arranging and every description possible for his appearances. By this point, everyone was into my new cyber boyfriend, living vicariously through me. Knowing I shouldn't write to him after three glasses of wine with girlfriends, I did anyway.

> Actually, I think the more we know about each other when we meet, the less strange it might be. I believe I have gotten to know you from your writing almost as well as I did light-years ago. I know you are sensitive, kind, generous, hardworking, and possibly a bit of a romantic—all wonderful attributes. It is very hard for me to believe you were not sent back into my life for a reason, dear friend. We shall see where this path leads and whether it will be like the river of years ago. Those are my thoughts on this rainy Monday night.

I ran a bath, filled it with oils and Epsom salt, and slipped in, my classical music streaming through the candlelit room. I closed my eyes as I remembered his, the bluest eyes I'd ever seen.

CHAPTER FORTY-FIVE

Inside Out

I AWOKE EARLY AND laced up my shoes for a quick walk before work. The humid air wrapped around me like a smothering blanket, so I shortened my usual route by a mile. I heard thunder in the distance and realized we were in for a wet day, the usual prediction for our Tallahassee summer. After a quick shower and blow dry, I was wearing my favorite yellow suit and newest heels. I would miss all the cute working clothes I had collected these last months. I thought I would deed them to my friend Jayne. She was my size, a professional, and had commented she liked them when we were together. We would build her wardrobe, especially since all the pieces were practically new.

I grabbed my purse and realized my car keys were missing. I started the hunt. Back in my office, I found them sitting on my desk. I hadn't checked my morning e-mail but remembered what I had written the night before after too much wine. I had no time to be reading e-mails but opened one of the three waiting from Dale. I glanced at the screen, still standing over my laptop. After his first two sentences, I sat down.

> I have never been the kind of person that wishes to dwell in the past, but rather I am the type of person that wishes to live for the future, remaining thankful for my past. Therefore, I am no longer sad about the end of our prior passions, nor am I trying to

> change our past. I am, and always have been, just happy for having had the chance to experience the brief time we had together. You made me happy then, and I have always been thankful for it. Because I consider happiness a gift, I forever treasure all the special things that remind me of my past happiness. Priscilla, that is why I continue to keep your gifts, the little oak memory box, and green flannel shirt.

I had to write him back, even if I would be late for work.

> You and I have much to learn about each other. A weekend will be nice. I never worried about the reconciliation of the past with the future. I believe we are guided by forces of power far greater than you or I will ever understand, and I have always believed that where it directs me, I will go. I believe they call that faith. So, a fun weekend is what I look forward to, especially seeing you again.

Even though two more e-mails remained unopened in my inbox, I ignored them and ran out the door. I worked through the day, wanting to open my personal e-mails from my workstation, dying to read what he wrote, but didn't. Instead, I stayed busy rifling applications—hundreds of them—looking for a qualified replacement, narrowing the selection for Frank's final decision. I had only fifteen more days before my last day. I had much to do.

Later that day, Kelly, one of Boone's sisters, invited the girls and me for dinner at her house. It was still hard, bittersweet, to spend time with the Kuersteiner family. All of them needed and wanted to talk about Boone, especially Garrett and Sara Britton. I had read books over the last months and learned people grieve differently. My way was to compartmentalize Boone, put him away safely in one area of my brain. My brain was easier to manipulate than my heart.

Their gathering and pulling out old videos and pictures, reflecting, and remembering, well, it was too painful for me. I knew I would never move forward if they kept pulling me back. I couldn't go there, no matter how much I wanted to. I felt I could never enjoy my life if I did that. I left feeling nostalgic, my fresh tears pooled despite the delicious dinner and their good intentions.

When I returned home, I showered and readied for bed. The two unopened e-mails from morning had grown to three. I settled in for my new ritual: reading and sipping my Sleepytime tea.

> Subject: Thirty-Year Reunion Hint 5
>
> One of the Landrum girls' names has significance in this town, as does Aaron's. Somewhere in Europe those two found each other in a crowd. To this city, as rivers go, the Big Blue River is far away, as is the Suwannee River.

Nope, still no clue. It had become worse than *Jeopardy!*. I realized he might be smarter than me. I opened the next e-mail:

> Subject: Thirty-Year Reunion Hint 6
>
> This city was founded as a fort in 1797. After 1862, it was an important Civil War Union Base, and today its population exceeds 600,000.

For the love of God, now he was using history for hints. Geography and history were two subjects I never liked. Give me a science or entertainment hint and I would get it. I decided I would tell him I was sick of hints and suggest he tell me where. Game over. I opened his last message before I shot off my snappy reply.

> Prissy, you are a very special lady. As your sisters said to you, God has set aside a special place just

> for you. Even though Boone's life was a short one, he was very fortunate and blessed to have married you. As I never thought I would ever see you again, for me our reunion will be a joyful experience I never imagined would occur. Worry not about the reconciliation of the past with the future, as I told you I have no expectations except we should meet again and have a wonderful time. The passage of time will take care of the rest, and with your blessing, young lady, that is exactly what I intend we do. I tried to choose a city for our meeting that would not distract us with old familiarities. I thought it best we not go to Indianapolis or Tallahassee as one or the other would then feel like they had to lead. There are only three more hints remaining.

The rain poured outside as I read every word, every line—three times. I didn't even know what he looked like, sounded like, or where I would be going to find out. I didn't care. I was 100 percent ready to go, anywhere. It was unimaginable for someone like me, yet it was true.

CHAPTER FORTY-SIX

Mystery Solved

I WOULD BE FLYING to Europe with my girlfriends only two days after I returned from my mystery reunion with Dale. Mary Ann, Julie, Linda, Lyn, and I got together to finalize our plans. The first week we would stay in London with Patti, who headed the study abroad program for FSU; she kept an apartment in the city during the summer months. The second week we planned to travel to the countryside. I was beyond ecstatic.

As we drank our chardonnay and shared summer cuisine, we plotted our museums, shops, and restaurants. I wanted to tell them about Dale. I started to but changed my mind. I didn't want anyone else's opinions. I feared they wouldn't endorse my spending an entire weekend with someone unknown to them, perhaps an axe murderer.

After dinner, back home again, I opened his newest e-mail, with another hint, as I suspected.

> Subject: Thirty-Year Reunion Hint 7
>
> PP and EAP were married for six years and then divorced. However, while together, they both graced this land by living in this town.

Finally, a language I understood: Hollywood, movie stars, artists, and singers. It was Memphis, Elvis and Priscilla Presley. I knew it and felt proud. Well, not too proud, since it had taken me seven hints to figure it out. Still, I immediately wrote him back.

> The mystery is over for me and hinting over for you. Memphis, am I right? I have never been to Memphis, how would you have known that? A perfect choice.

It was only a few weeks until we were to meet. I went to bed excited about both trips—England and Memphis—unsure which took lead.

Rolling over the next morning, I realized we had a plan, jumped out of bed, and checked my electronic mailbox. There he was, my early riser cyber guy.

> Good morning. You having never been there either, well, it really makes me happy. When you assigned this arranger job to me, it was one of my first criteria. I wanted us to meet again where neither of us had ever been, as I thought a past might muddy the emotional waters. Yesterday, I think I determined which crowd we shall find each other in. However, don't ask me. I am not hinting or telling you anything about it. At the last minute, you shall find out where that is. Also, don't ask about the stockholder or travel arrangements or clothes or this or that or whatever, as you gave me the arranger job and I promise you I will take care of it.

I was growing more excited but waited to write. I still had my Doncaster Fashion Consultant calling card, the designer clothing company I had been working for for the last twenty-five years. Beverly, my partner, and I were having the summer collection at my house the following week. Appointments had been scheduled for nights, after my work hours, and the upcoming weekend. I had clothes to unpack, inventory to check, displays to coordinate, and clothes to sell. Plus, I had found the perfect person to take my job and had only thirteen more workdays until my job with Frank ended. I was euphorically manic.

It was midnight before I finally responded:

> It sounds like you are planning an itinerary, so here is a taste of me. I like all sorts of foods, seldom watch television, mostly listen to music, read, or exercise. I think you might wear me out by the end of our weekend, and I will be a zombie when I travel to Europe two days later. Who knows, if this is a success, you may need a passport yourself.

I couldn't believe what I wrote, assuming our weekend would be perfect, never entertaining the notion it could be anything but. Suggesting he might need a passport was ridiculous; I was embarrassed in front of my own self. Too late to worry, I put it out of my Pollyanna mind.

Between my clothing show, work, and finalizing all my travel arrangements and frocks for Europe, my job jar was spilling over. Still, I wanted to spend extra time with my girls. I took Puddles over to my girls' house to visit her siblings, Pooh and Belle.

Puddles loved running around with the girls' dogs. I had bought Belle as a Christmas present for Sara Britton during one of my weaker moments. The dog, a huge standard poodle, was crazy wild and needed Ritalin from the first day. I was glad she was tearing up their yard and not mine.

It felt good having the three of us nestled together, watching a cooking show, and catching up. We made plans to spend Fourth of July weekend at our beach house, and I shared my excitement about my upcoming London trip. They were more interested in Memphis. Aware of Garrett's skeptical gaze, I played it down, but she wanted every detail and continued to interrogate.

"Leave her alone, Garrett," Sara Britton snapped.

"I don't get it. Why won't he come here if he wants to see you?" Garrett asked.

"It's more fun this way, finding each other in a crowd," I said, shrugging.

"Yeah, well, you could have done that here," she said.

I realized our conversation wasn't going the way she wanted. But I enjoyed the game of hints with Dale, plus I wanted to meet him *before* I introduced him to either of the girls, though I didn't tell them that. So I changed the subject and asked about their boyfriends, both of them being in serious relationships by then. It worked.

Before heading back home, Puddles and I stopped by my mother's house so Puddles could play with her two Yorkie pups, Rhett and Scarlett. I sat with Mom on her terrace, watching her little fur balls run around.

As I visited with my mother that afternoon, I felt lucky. She was happy, healthy, still beautiful, and had become content with her new life in Tallahassee. My whole family lived within five miles of each other: my mother, two sisters and their families, and my two daughters. Like Garrett, my mother couldn't understand my plans to fly to Memphis to meet Dale, suggesting more than once he should be flying to Tallahassee. I changed the subject with her too. *Where is the adventure in these people who love me?* I thought as I drove to my empty house.

Everything was just as I left it that morning, spotless and neurotically clean. I turned on some music, headed for my favorite space—my office—and searched my in-box. He never disappointed. There it was.

> Now that you know the city, FedEx will deliver a package to Carriage Road that will arrive four days before the 16th of July. You will then know how you shall travel. FedEx will make another delivery the next day, three days before the 16th of the July. You will then know the holder.

I reread it again, still confused. Tickets and a holder, hum, still some suspense going on with the guy. I laughed and headed off to the kitchen to find some supper.

CHAPTER FORTY-SEVEN

Book and Cover

IT WAS THE FOLLOWING week, and I slipped from my office to meet Nancy and Gayle for lunch at a downtown restaurant, Andrews Down Under. Both of them commented on the glow I wore.

"You look great. I haven't seen you look so happy in forever. What's going on?" Gayle asked.

"She only has a week left to work, that's what's going on," Nancy said between bites of Caesar salad.

"Yeah, that makes me happy, but I'm excited about London too."

"You still meeting that guy first?" Gayle asked.

"Yep, the weekend before, and for the umpteenth time, his name is Dale."

"I don't know why I can't remember that name," she said.

"Because you aren't trying. It should be easy, since it rhymes with your name. You still think I'm making a mistake meeting him," I said a bit too curtly.

"I've been thinking about it some more. It might be fun, especially since you've been writing," Gayle admitted. "I still don't get why he never married, though. It's weird. I'm sorry, it just is."

"She'll find out why when she sees him in Memphis and he weighs four hundred pounds," Nancy said, laughing and simultaneously blotting her lipstick. "For the record, I'm excited, though. Can't wait to hear every single detail."

Better than the skipped dessert, I had two from my village coming around to my side after all. I wrote him later that evening.

> My entire crew knows I am meeting you. I'm beginning to think the entire village may know before long. Some of them aren't too excited, can I just tell you? And yet, you have told no one. Why is that? Perhaps it's because you're afraid of what they'll say. Something like—didn't she break your heart once? Why are you meeting her after all these years, she may do it again.

I hit send. I hoped he was reading. I waited for his reply.

> No one would say that about you, since I never told them anything about our path-splitting history in the first place. I am brave enough, believe me, I asked myself that question before I ever wrote you the second time. I don't need courage for your village people. They don't scare me. However, I do need courage for many other reasons, and like I said, I am brave enough.

I gave his reply some thought before answering.

> I have raised my girls with my beliefs: choose wisely through your wisdom. The old saying "never chose a book by its cover" has been pounded into their heads. Covers fade and tear, but contents of that book hold a message. I decided to read a few paragraphs of your book and that's why I really didn't want to see or talk to you at first. Many times, it would have been very easy to pick up the phone and call or scan pictures. I wanted to see if this book was articulately written, funny, romantic,

> mysterious, and full of some meaning. When I discovered it was—you were—that's when I decided to meet you.

I waited an hour, and when he never wrote back, I went to bed wondering. I should have remembered he wasn't a night owl like me.

The next morning, my returned e-mail was waiting, delivered at 3:45 a.m. *Ridiculous, insane, to be up at that time writing e-mails*, I thought.

He wrote,

> I don't think of myself as a romantic or sensitive. You blew me away when you said that. I told you, this is all new to me, this social writing thing. I had no idea you were such a book critic either. I'm glad I passed the test. Your review came at just the right time, as this book has been evolving for nearly three months now and I was growing impatient. I hope, as the author of this book, I can live up to your good review. Additionally, once you see the book's cover, I hope you are reasonably satisfied. As we both would agree, a good book with a pleasing cover is preferable.

When Fourth of July weekend came, I decided to leave my laptop at home and spend the next four days with my family, giving them my undivided attention. I invited everyone to our beach house to join the girls and me for Fourth celebrations: boyfriends, my mom, and my sisters and their families. It was breezy, festive, delicious, and revealing. Dale was the center of conversation, my sisters and mother telling my girls everything they wanted to know. After all, they remembered well this boy with blue eyes who spent days, weeks, months, and years hanging around Montgomery Drive. It was a fascinating, reflective celebration for me and not because it was July Fourth.

CHAPTER FORTY-EIGHT

Freedom Shrine

A FEW DAYS AFTER July Fourth celebrations, it was my last day at the governor's office. I was surprised when I arrived at work and found my office colleagues had thrown me a party including better-than-sex chocolate cake, balloons, friendly cheer, and complimentary toasts. I had shared my upcoming mystery reunion and European adventure with most of them. There were a few jokes about the prospect of later finding my body in a dumpster somewhere in Memphis. One staffer likened my reunion to a Match.com weekend.

The party was a generous gesture and statement of appreciation; I was humbled by the attention. Still, I was secretly embarrassed, as though I was abandoning the ship. I'd found a perfect replacement for Frank. Her name was Leslie, and she happened to be the mother of Matt, Sara Britton's boyfriend. Frank knew Matt, having met him once before interviewing his mother for the job. Frank had commented on Matt's politeness the day he met him.

I responded with the usual remark I gave affirming children with good manners: "He has a good mother, and she raised him well." I was lucky to have found her application and presented it to Frank as my first suggestion. I knew she would be a perfect match for Frank. She was a hard worker, attractive, and overqualified.

After the party was over at the day's end, I started collecting my personal things from my cubicle. I picked up the picture of Boone and me, inside my favorite ornate frame, which sat front and center on the wooden desk. I looked at the two of us with awkward smiles, the picture taken in the lobby of the Cloister on the weekend of our twenty-fifth wedding anniversary. I studied it momentarily, remembering, then wrapped it in paper towels and laid it on top of the other paraphernalia in the box. I wiped my desk off with the furniture polish I had stored in my purse that morning, stood back, and approved of my overzealous cleaning.

I had one more thing to do before I left the building for the last time. I walked the corridor to the staircase and climbed the twenty-two flights of stairs. When I reached the twenty-second floor, I walked out to the observation deck with its panoramic view. It was a clear, cloudless day with a cerulean blue sky. I gazed south, toward the almost visible coastline so many miles away, and back again at the south wall displaying the collection of Freedom Shrine documents. I smiled and hoped it was just one more sign.

Later, as I celebrated my retirement with girlfriends, each of them, one after another, poked fun at the longevity of my short-lived employment. I gave them an update on my most recent e-mails from Dale.

"Suppose you like him. What good is it if he lives a thousand miles away?" Bunny asked.

"Yeah, would you ever move there?" Jayne chimed in.

Those were two questions I hadn't even considered. How could I have a relationship with someone so far away? What was I thinking? I realized I hadn't thought about it much. I worried on the drive back home, later sending an e-mail mentioning the distance between us. His response came the next day.

> I would be less than honest if I didn't admit I have had similar thoughts about the 1,000 miles. However, for me, the distance has almost made it more

> exciting than it would have been if I lived there, and that is a fact. Prissy, as I have said, I have only two expectations: one, we meet again, and two, we have a wonderful time. I feel no pressure from everyone's expectations, and I believe no matter what happens it will be for the best. Again, you have been the focal point of another wonderful moment in my life, as I have truly enjoyed what we have done over the last three months. I will never forget this time, and that is a fact. I believe our renewed friendship has helped us both. Whatever happens, beyond friendship, time will tell, and I am not concerned about that. I look forward to it this time; the worse we must let it be is friendship. I am older and much more mature. I am not the lovesick puppy you once knew.

I wrote back,

> I have digested and you are 100% right in everything you said. Fun is waiting in Memphis and that is all there is to it.

I slept fitfully that night, tossing and turning. I woke up regretful, angry, and disappointed in myself. It was reckless to have quit my job, and it was overindulgent to be spending money flying to Europe with friends who had husbands paying their way. I was living out of character. I wondered if this was a delayed reaction to losing Boone. He had always controlled my life. Maybe I was proving to everyone—even me—no one would control me, not ever again.

With no job to get ready for, I took a long walk, but the heat and humidity of July drove me back home. I decided to send Dale a longer e-mail, an addendum to the previous night's one line. I found another e-mail waiting before I could.

> Question: will you be home next Monday and Tuesday? Please let me know as it is important to

> the development of the reunion plot. If you aren't, then give me an alternate. It doesn't need to be all day, just in the morning, say, up until noon.

I settled in and wrote,

> Will I be home on Monday or Tuesday? If I should, I will. I've been wondering how you have changed. I never really thought about it until today. You know, how you look. Is that not strange? Anyway, it felt strange, I don't know why. Did you shave your beard? I had horrible dreams last night, one involved me drowning. I'm feeling shaky today because of it. I'm one of those people who believe in signs, bad and good. Guess you should know that about me.

Moments later I had an e-mail. Clearly he wasn't running his company but rather waiting for my e-mail.

> In one of your earlier e-mails, you remember asking if I was fat, bald, and had yellow teeth? You already knew the answers, didn't you? Otherwise, you would not have asked. You have thought about it before yesterday, so admit it. I have thought about it too, and I imagine you have changed very little. From what I have read, you most likely are as beautiful as ever, maybe even more beautiful than I remember. I never was beautiful. If you don't already know how I look, I believe you will be really surprised.
>
> I was happy to hear I didn't frighten you in my last e-mail; that's great as I know a little more about my old girlfriend now. May you have better dreams tonight, maybe you can dream about knights on white horses rescuing you from dragons.

That night I slept like a baby.

CHAPTER FORTY-NINE

Planes and Stockholder

IT WAS THE MORNING of July 12, and I had assured Dale I would be home between ten and noon. I spent my time cleaning and primping, secretly wondering if he might surprise me and show up at my door.

At ten thirty, I heard the doorbell ring. Honestly, I felt like Cinderella, expecting to have the prince and his entourage holding my glass slipper. It was a crazy thought, but Dale was unpredictable. I was disappointed to find just a nice, friendly, sign-on-the-dotted-line FedEx guy. I tore open the envelope and read Dale's note.

> In this FedEx, I have enclosed your plane tickets. An enclosed itinerary, also provided, identifies the origin of your journey to be Tallahassee, beginning on Friday the 16th at 10:10 a.m. Prissy, I remain excited and will truly enjoy the remainder of our wait. I hope your trip to Memphis is a pleasant and memorable one. I know mine will be.

The plane ticket was first class. Holy cow, he wasn't sparing any expense trying to woo me. Dale had certainly upgraded from his life once lived in a camper trailer. I was impressed, not with the first-class ticket, but the man who gifted it. Good for him. He was a great arranger and very romantic. Funny, I didn't remember him romantic. Still, I had this nagging feeling. What if he was expecting too much? The feeling hung on throughout the day, excitement coupled with fear. I didn't want to hurt him. When reading his e-mails, I always felt sure and looked forward to our reuniting. But when I talked to other people, those skeptical of my romantic rendezvous, their negativity fed my self-doubt. I suppressed my fluctuating emotions as I readied myself for two trips.

I began to realize that trying to squeeze in a weekend to Memphis two days before leaving for Europe was a ridiculous decision. I would have only one day to unpack, repack, and tie up all the loose ends, but it was too late to change plans.

The next day, as requested, I hung around the house waiting for another piece of Dale's hinting puzzle.

I had no idea why anyone would spend the extra money sending two different items—next-day air, no less—only one day apart. He could have combined the two. In just the few last days, I had uncovered some characteristics about Dale I hadn't known. He was creative, organized, generous, and awfully extravagant.

At 11:15 a.m., the doorbell rang. This time I didn't expect a prince at my front door; I was pretty sure it would just be the second FedEx he told me to expect. Just as I had the day before, I signed then tore open the new envelope. Inside I found a letter with a picture labeled "Mike." I read the letter.

> Prissy,
>
> The enclosed picture is Mike, a friend who owns stock in my company. Mike and his family live in Memphis, and consequently, he is the stockholder that will show you the way.
>
> Mike will greet you as you deplane and escort you to the Peabody Hotel, where you and I will lodge. Your room has been prearranged so when you arrive everything will already have been taken care of. I have

> asked Mike not to answer any questions about my appearance or the sound of my voice. I asked him not to tell me anything about yours, as I want both of us to be surprised. Mike will be carrying a special piece of identification, and when you see him, you will know for sure he is waiting for you. This identification will erase all doubts, as he has been instructed to give it to you.
> Dale

I wanted to call Dale and break our e-mail only agreement, but instead, I used my overzealous excitement and called everyone else: Sara Britton, Gayle, Nancy, Deborah, Gina, my mother, and Garrett. My first-class ticket and weekend at the Peabody, along with the method of delivery, elevated my mystery man in all of their minds. Perhaps—I hoped—even Garrett, who happened to be the biggest skeptic of them all.

Later, I wrote,

> I am delighted not to have to ride the Greyhound with all the ex-convicts, though I would have—maybe. Your organizational skills are incredible, and when I read them to my sister Deborah, she said you remind her of me. Seriously, I appreciate all your hard work planning this gathering. The Peabody is a great choice. Yes, you are a real romantic, and don't think otherwise, as your secret is out now. By the way, you did not have to fly me first class; it only contributes to my charmed life. Thank you.

An hour later, I got his reply:

> Now tell me, could I have flown first class and you not? Some more about me, I am the kind of person that would rather wait until I can go first class rather than settle for second.

I had to answer, though my day's to-do list still had nothing scratched off.

> Thank God you are a first-class guy, as I was a little worried. You are the fellow who dragged me around to every trailer park in Lake City, trying so hard to make me believe they were wonderful. I almost did, you know.

Two days before Memphis, I was busy figuring out what to pack for my weekend. It looked like I had headless mannequins all over my bed. Each of my five outfits laid out in matched detail, down to the shoes and jewelry. I answered the ringing phone, studying the ensemble spread everywhere. It was Shirley, a friend, client, and the person who shared my mailing address with Dale before he sent the sympathy card. She had attended the Doncaster summer trunk collection at my house two weeks earlier.

"I need to return the black skirt," she told me. "It's just too big I think. Can I drop it by your house on Friday?"

"Gosh, I'm leaving town on Friday, so Monday is better. Would that work?" I asked.

"Where are you going? Someplace fun I hope."

"Actually, I'm going to Memphis, meeting Dale."

There was a pause.

"Shirley, are you still there?"

"I'm here. You're *meeting* Dale? Why?" Her tone was less friendly now, almost angry.

I was surprised by the question, so I told her about his sympathy card, our three months of writing, no phone calls or pictures, and our plan to meet in Memphis and pick each other from a crowd.

"Do you know how you broke his heart, Prissy? Do you have any idea what you did to him, how he's pined for you all these years? You will destroy him if you do that again. He is one of the nicest men I've ever known. You have nothing in common, *nothing*."

I was speechless.

What I always liked most about Shirley was her frankness. She and Dale had attended the University of West Florida in Pensacola at the same time. She knew firsthand things I hadn't known or didn't know. Her intentions were good, her worry for Dale genuine. I admired her gumption in sharing her thoughts and concerns. I hung up and no longer cared what I packed. I had bigger problems. What had I done to the blue-eyed boy I once loved? Even worse, what was I doing now?

CHAPTER FIFTY

Heavy Weight

AFTER THE BRIEF PHONE call with Shirley, I stewed. As the day went on, I decided to forget about the phone call and worry later about all the stuff Shirley had said. The closer Dale and I came to meeting, the more flirtatious our e-mail exchanges became. I decided to tone it down but only because of what Shirley told me.

Knowing I'd be out of town for several weeks, I resolved to spend time cleaning the refrigerator, discarding perishables and scrubbing the shelves, doors, and interior. My annoying trait—overcleaning—was in overdrive. As aggravating as it was, the mechanics of the process kept my mind from wandering to the what-ifs regarding Dale: no chemistry, no attraction, no fun, and no e-mailing partner. I enjoyed his correspondence. I would miss that, for sure.

By mid-afternoon, the fridge was done and I needed a break. I made a pitcher of fresh iced tea, tossed in some mint, and settled in my desk chair and found a new e-mail waiting for me.

> What are you crowd-wearing? Knowing would make it easier on me. No, don't tell me, and I won't tell you. I remember Shalimar. All you must do is get close to me. If you want anything else from this arranger, you must tell me soon, as the next thing you know we will be face-to-face. I will check my

> mail this afternoon, so it is your last chance to give me more orders.

I typed my response:

> No requests from me. I am an easy girl (no, not that kind), please don't work yourself up trying to find entertainment. In case you are nervous, you should realize this meeting is the equivalent of four months of dating. Throw in the three years you knew me before, and you have longevity. See you in Memphis.

That was that. The next communication between us would be face-to-face, for better or worse. *Lord, Prissy, what have you gotten yourself into?* I wondered.

Even though I kept trying to push every word Shirley said out of my mind, I couldn't. How could Dale have—what was the word she used—*pined* for me for thirty years? I never believed Chip that time he told me Dale never got over me. Chip and Shirley told the same story, though. There must be some sliver of truth.

That evening, Garrett and Sara Britton came over for a fashion meeting or, rather, a wardrobe coup, worried what I might wear, witnessing some of my latest "going-out" clothes. So they had me try on multiple outfits and model them around the bedroom. They voted among themselves and selected my perfect "reuniting" ensemble. I spent the next twenty-four hours worrying about Dale, Shirley, and my e-mail shenanigans. The weight on my shoulders was heavier than my packed suitcase.

I sat in the first-class cabin, wearing my white linen slacks, olive tank top, a chunky gold necklace, gold loop earrings, and strappy bronze sandals. My suntanned skin, after weekends at the beach, looked even darker against the white and olive ensemble. I had the very same asymmetrical, stacked hairstyle I had in college.

Clearly, I needed to step out of the box when it came to hairstyles.

Tucked in my carry-on bag were old and new photographs, all requested by Dale. He wanted to acquaint and reacquaint himself with my children, my mom, my late dad, Deborah, Gina, and of course, Mazelle.

We were over an hour late leaving Atlanta—my connecting hub—making me more nervous and chatty. The poor executive who sat next to me whose name was Bob asked what took me to Memphis. By landing time, he knew the whole story, starting with Boone, ending with Dale. Bob finished four screwdrivers before the wheels were released for landing and asked for my phone number to learn how it ended in Memphis. For the record, I had only two screwdrivers but probably, definitely, should have been served only one.

By the time the plane taxied to the gate, we were fifty minutes late. Before deplaning, I refreshed my perfume and lipstick and then creamed my hands and feet. Bob was too drunk to notice.

As I exited the plane and walked the corridor to the gate lobby, I heard clapping and cheering from the people all gathered in the waiting area. I assumed they were glad the plane finally arrived, tired of waiting for their own departure. I looked around for Mike—the stockholder mentioned in the hint—who would have "identification" I would recognize.

He walked up holding an old picture of Dale and me. I was dressed in my prom dress from 1968, wearing a homemade shocking pink chiffon dress, a glued rhinestone necklace attached at the neckline. The matching pink-dyed Baker heels sealed the outfit. My beaming smile showcased the $1,000 orthodontic bill my father paid. Dale stood next to me in the photo, looking just as I remembered him as I tapped away my messages night after night.

"Hey, I'm Mike. Welcome to Memphis, Prissy." He tried to shake my hand, but I leaned in to give him my Southern hug.

"Sorry," he said, laughing. "While we've all hung here waiting for the plane, I told some folks the story of you guys meeting again. They were helping me find you from this picture."

I was completely caught off guard as the clapping went on, everyone watching as Mike and I hugged and exchanged greetings. Several of the waiting passengers walked over to say they loved the story, wished me luck, and hoped it ended well. Each one of them a stranger, each one wanting to believe in a happily-ever-after fairy-tale ending. I felt like a celebrity.

But afterward, my reservations intensified and my second-guessing reared its ugly head as we drove from the airport toward the Peabody. I wanted to meet Dale. I did. He seemed to be everything I remembered and more. But what if he wasn't? What if I wasn't attracted to him, or what if we had nothing in common once we reunited? What could I do to keep from hurting him yet again? How could I bow out gracefully, or worse, could I? I almost felt trapped. I forced myself to push all the questions out of my mind and remembered what he had written early on in the planning stage: "Whatever happens, beyond friendship, time will tell, and I am not concerned about that. I look forward to it this time; the worse we must let it be is friendship. I am older and much more mature. I am not the lovesick puppy you once knew."

Lord, I hoped he meant it. I started to get excited again as we sped along the highway from the airport toward downtown Memphis.

CHAPTER FIFTY-ONE

Be Still My Heart

AS WE TURNED ONTO Union Avenue, I saw the red neon letters spelling out "The Peabody" atop the classic 1920s building. My heart fluttered. Mike parked the car, and as I stepped out, the blistering rays from the hot noon sun beamed down onto my sleeveless arms. Mike pulled my suitcase from the trunk of his small, sporty car. He was a man with few words, so the *only* conversation on our ride from the airport came from me, fueled by my two screwdrivers in flight. Mike escorted me through the Peabody lobby at a quickened pace. There was no stopping at the front desk for my room key; apparently, he already had it. I trailed behind him, distracted by the mallard ducks—beautiful hens and drakes—swimming in the lobby fountain as spectators gathered to admire them. Mike called out my name as he stood holding the elevator door open. I wondered if Dale was nearby watching us.

Once inside the elevator, Mike inserted the room key and pushed the twelfth-floor button, explaining how the key insertion worked for club-level floors. I pretended to be impressed, as though I had never used an elevator with private-floor access before.

The heat, humidity, and travel, coupled with my early morning alcohol, had caused my fingers to swell. I looked at my hands and realized I still had on my wedding ring: three individual diamonds, a carat each, set in its own Tiffany setting. I meant to leave the ring in Tallahassee. It was extravagant, a bit opulent, but I loved it. I still wore it every day even though Boone had been gone for sixteen months. I thought I caught a peripheral glimpse of Mike staring at my hand, so I twisted my ring around, making only the gold back of the ring visible. We were both nervous—him, perhaps more. His brow beaded with perspiration.

As we stood in front of Room 1214, Mike swiped the keycard and opened the door. He motioned me ahead and carried in my suitcase. I looked around the spacious and elegant suite, its color scheme a silver blue coupled with bronze. It had a historical, Renaissance flavor, with white and gold matching furniture. Mike could tell I was impressed.

"Yeah, I know," he said, smiling. "Old Dale didn't spare any expense on you, Prissy. I sure hope you guys have a great weekend, I really do. It's great to finally meet you."

"Nice to meet you too, Mike. Thanks for picking me up."

We hugged and he left.

I stood by the door, still admiring the capacious suite, then headed to the bathroom and found it just as magnificent, gigantic, with cream marble. I was so enamored with the striking surroundings I missed seeing the massive flower arrangement sitting on the desk in the separate living room. There were several dozen red roses, artfully arranged, their fragrant scent filling the air in both rooms of the suite. I located the card tucked inside the flowers and recognized Dale's handwriting.

> Thirty red roses, one for each of the years since we last met
> Two handmade baskets with special stuffing from me
> A mystery envelope from Carole
> And another blue one for after five
> Also, directions to our crowd
> A few more hours and we shall see
> Prissy-Prissy-Prissy
> I sure hope you enjoy the Peabody

I saw a sealed envelope and opened it, hoping it might reveal where and when we were meeting.

> Prissy,
>
> The crowd I have chosen for us is the "Peabody Duck Crowd." Each day at 5:00 p.m., the ducks return to their "Royal Duck Palace." They will waddle down the red carpet to the elevator, and in this crowd, you and I will find each other. If you have not found me, or I you, by 5:00 p.m., please open the blue envelope and read the highlighted paragraph. Please do not open it until then and before 5:00 p.m. Keep the envelope sealed; otherwise, I would have the picking advantage. I will arrive in the lobby sometime before 5:00 and your time of arrival is up to you. If we can't find one another by 5:30, just call me on my mobile and then we can talk our way together.
>
> You will have some time to pass before the crowd assembles so I have provided some things I thought you might enjoy. These I have placed on your bed, please use whatever you like of them. It is your choice, do whatever you like, and to make it easy, I have also provided a list of things available in the Peabody. Don't worry about running into me before the crowd assembles, I will be elsewhere until then. Just relax, enjoy, and after all this time we will finally meet again.
>
> Dale

I looked toward the oversized bed. On top of the blue silk comforter were two large gift baskets. The first one, a handmade Nantucket basket, was filled with all types of niceties: lavender soap, lemon bubble bath, coconut body lotion, and more, all the items creatively arranged then wrapped in a big organza bow. The other basket held a collection of carefully selected miniature books. I read the titles: *In Praise of Moms*; *Love, Quotations from the Heart*, a poetry collection; and *Aries*, my zodiac sign, along with some Memphis tourist literature and current ladies' magazines.

Dale could not have lavished me more: flowers, baskets, books, and potions—not to mention, the elegant suite. It seemed clear he had placed all the chosen treasures inside my room himself, probably while Mike was fetching me from the airport. I smiled thinking about it, wishing I had been a fly on the wall observing as he moved the flowers around and tried to find the perfect place.

It was only twelve thirty, and we weren't meeting until five. I was starving. More than that, I was suddenly disappointed. I was wearing my adorable meet-and-greet outfit, painfully chosen by my two girls. Now we weren't meeting until the end of the day, so he wouldn't see it. And whom was I supposed to eat lunch with?

I looked through the basket of books and found Dale had made a list of suggested restaurants along Beale Street. I thought about going to one but decided he could be lurking, so I didn't want to take the chance. Instead, I looked over the room service menu and ordered a BLT and iced tea.

While I waited for their quoted forty-five-minute delivery, I opted to shower any airport germs that had hitchhiked in transit. I tore the cellophane from the expertly wrapped basket and pulled out lemon soap and coconut cream, stuffed my already-styled hair into a shower cap, and climbed into the oversized shower.

After my white-tablecloth lunch and feeling overstuffed, I pulled a bottle of well-chilled Chardonnay from the minibar and poured myself a glass. I needed to settle the butterflies gathering in my stomach. It was only two o'clock, still three hours until we were to meet.

To pass the time, I used the hotel phone and started dialing: Sara Britton first, then Garrett, Gayle, my mother, both of my sisters, and finally Du. I told them everything from the beginning: the airport greeting, my gorgeous suite, the thirty roses, my two gift baskets holding all the goodies, his note with the roses, and finally, the letter instructing me to meet him among the ducks.

Then it dawned on me. Verbally exhausted from sharing the news, I realized the lunch expense and all those phone calls would be on Dale's tab. I was momentarily embarrassed but quickly realized it was trivial compared to my first-class plane ticket and the cushiony bed inside my palatial suite, where I lay curled up.

One hour later, I decided to find another outfit to wear. I pulled clothes from my suitcase and started trying things on, one by one. I stood on the bed for a better view from the mirror across the room. I turned around and checked myself from behind. I had narrowed down the second-round first-impression ensemble between two outfits: a brown sundress with yellow polka dots and a black tank top with black silk pants. I chose the sundress, thinking it would show off my legs. Then I decided pants might serve me better, less flesh showing, as I did not want to encourage Dale should I find myself not attracted to him. I needed a girlfriend's opinion on my dilemma. I called Nancy.

"What do you think—black pants and top or brown and yellow sundress?" I asked.

"Definitely the sundress. You'll look like Julia Roberts in *Pretty Woman*. It's just like the one she wore to the race." She laughed.

"Yeah, well, her lips are fuller, she's at least eight inches taller, and her hair is much longer. I don't think I can look like her."

"At least you have the same color hair and eyes. You got that going for you. Don't forget too, her white knight climbed the balcony and rescued her; yours might ride the Peabody elevator."

We were still laughing when I hung up. I was more relaxed, plus I finally knew what to wear.

Nancy and her husband were two of my biggest Dale supporters. Not even knowing him, they loved our history. They were high school sweethearts and had been married over thirty years.

It was four thirty, and I was wired, too nervous to wait thirty more minutes. I decided I would head to the upper mezzanine level then look below to the lobby and see if I saw Dale among the duck gatherers waiting for the ceremonial march to the elevator.

The sundress, with its yellow dots against the bronze silk fabric, showed off my Florida tan. My recently highlighted hair smelled like coconut after I discarded my shower cap and washed my hair *again* with the yummy shampoo left in my gift basket from Dale.

My heart raced as I walked off the elevator and looked around the spacious mezzanine level. It was vacant, quiet, and enormous. There was not one soul on the floor where I stood. I walked toward the brass railing and heard the chatter of distant voices, children's laughter, and festive blues music rising from below. I looked over the railing and realized the mezzanine was vacant because everyone was downstairs.

There must have been over a hundred people waiting. They mingled and watched the ducks splashing or gracefully skimming the fountain water. I studied the top of every man's head. There were so many people: men, women, children, full heads, bald heads, brunettes, and blondes. I had no idea whom I was looking for or what he looked like.

Picking him from the mezzanine level wouldn't work. I needed to go downstairs, I decided, and bent down to grab my purse. As I rose, I felt a tap on my shoulder and turned around. There he stood, right in front of me, the only other person on the mezzanine level.

We stood less than three feet apart, just staring. His piercing blue eyes blinked then misted with tears. I stepped toward him, and my head reached only as high as his chest. I laid my cheek against his silk shirt damp with his anxious perspiration, and his arms wrapped around me. I inhaled his once familiar scent through the fabric brushing my skin and listened to his rapid heartbeat. We stood unmoving, as memories embedded for years flooded every cell of my body. Without either of us speaking a single word, I already knew. I was home.

to be continued . . .

Acknowledgments

There are so many people who helped bring this story to you by encouraging me to write it.

I want to thank my friend Gayle, who insisted that I should keep a journal on the yellow ledger she planted on my kitchen desk. There were days I couldn't, or wouldn't, pick up a pen. As I began writing this memoir, I found Gayle's handwriting scribbled on my coffee-stained pages.

Spider, thank you for visiting Boone even when he didn't know you were there, and Bobby, thank you for the special Subway lunches. To Phoebe, Beverly, Lyn, Fred, Alex, Diane, Bill, Bunny, and Jayne, thank you a thousand times. There were so many in our beautiful Tallahassee village who watched over us during those dark months. The devotion was palpable and will always remain embedded in my heart.

Thank you to Rhonda Baldock for leading the team of culinary angels. All those months, we were showered with benevolent nourishment. My heartfelt thanks to our Carriage Road neighbors and those who cooked and delivered.

A grateful heart to David and KD Inge; Carole and Jim Smith; and Boone's law firm, Greenberg Traurig, for love and support before, during, and afterward.

Georgia Smith, thank you for sharing your alternative research. Fellow Lake City girl Betsy Pottle, thank you for insisting

I needed to breathe sea air; you were right.

To Boone's seven brothers and sisters—Dick, Karol Ann, Kris, Clay, Kelly, Kurt, and Katia—and to my sister Deborah and her husband, Karl; my sister Gina; Chip; and my mother, Sylvia, thank you for your endless love and support.

Mike Robinson and Matt Jacobs, thank you for loving my beautiful girls and caring for them when I couldn't.

Nancy, dear gym-rat friend, thank you for rejecting *all* my excuses and making me exercise and get healthy again. I loved our Tae Bo days.

Elda Martinko and Shirley McFadden, thank you for your help in guiding Dale back to me. There are no words for your role in my happiness.

To every caregiver reading this, I wish you courage, strength, and faith. God *is* merciful, even when you have doubts and are in your darkest hours. My lifelong gratitude to Cornelius Duhart, Sallie Madison Duhart, Mazelle Patterson, the late Willie Stokes, and the late Betty Jones. You will be loved forevermore.

Thanks to Barbara Hogan for telling me I *could* write this memoir, along with Hollis Gillispie and her Kick-Ass Boot Camp (it's really called that). It gave me the kick that helped me finish what I started.

Another thank-you to my Wisdom Writing Group: Beverly, Judy, Maria, Marie, and Betty, all great writers, now friends.

Steve Adams, a Pushcart Prize–winning author, manuscript evaluator, and copyeditor, a big ol' thank you for sharing your talent and complementing mine. And my hat is off to Jennifer Zaczek, my proof editor, interior designer, and formatting genius. Thank you for polishing and honing *Far Outside the Ordinary* with such scrutiny and for all your excellent suggestions.

Katie Campbell, my cover designer who oozes talent, thank you for your patience in helping to translate this story graphically. I knew you would make me proud. You did.

A big thank-you to LeAnne Gibbs, a beautiful, smart, thirty-four-year-old widow who I was lucky enough to meet a few weeks after I completed this memoir. No one understands caregiving and widowhood like another widow. Age is irrelevant. We believe our paths crossed, perhaps, through divine intervention. After reading the following page about Fresh New Start, a nonprofit she started for young widows with children, you might agree. Thank you, LeAnne, and may all your dreams come true. You, too, will one day live happily ever after, just in a different way than you once expected.

And last, but definitely first, I want to thank Dale, Garrett, and Sara Britton for waiting patiently—three years—to read a word of my manuscript. I had to muster enough courage to share my thoughts, words, sentences, paragraphs, and chapters that formed this book. Your tears, praise, and the love bestowed after reading *Far Outside the Ordinary* engulfed my heart. In the end, it's all that really mattered.

LeAnne Gibbs became a cancer widow at the age of 34. Her husband of six years and father to their two children, Francis, was diagnosed with adenocarcinoma of the colon on May 12, 2012, and a year after diagnosis, he passed away on May 17, 2013.

Francis wished for LeAnne to take a trip with a few girlfriends to refresh and renew herself as she restarted a life without him.

A few months after his death, LeAnne took the trip Francis requested. His wish is one LeAnne believes could help other young cancer widows. Since Francis' passing, LeAnne has dedicated herself to providing support to young cancer widows. She founded Fresh New Start, a nonprofit organization that provides encouragement and support to young women who have lost their husbands to cancer.

If you would like to learn more about Fresh New Start's mission, visit www.freshnewstart.org; if you know a young cancer widow, encourage her to contact mail@freshnewstart.org.